Roger Burggraeve SDB

Amorevolezza, Ragione, Religione

Kindness, Reason, Religion

Holistic Education for Today in the Footsteps of Don Bosco

Don Bosco Publications
Thornleigh House, Sharples Park, Bolton BL1 6PQ
United Kingdom

ISBN 978-1-909080-90-4

Front cover illustration @sdb.org

Printed in the Uk by Jump DP

Acknowledgements

In grateful memory of a brotherly companion and dialogue partner:
Julien Jackers SDB (1945–2021)

Copyright Acknowledgement

Contents

Introduction

There are two well-known perspectives to understand and interpret the pedagogical concept of Don Bosco. On the one hand, the binary idea of a repressive versus a preventive system and, on the other, the triple concept of 'kindness, reason, religion' (*amorevolezza, ragione, religione*). The analysis and deepening of these three dimensions, which also evoke essential dynamics of human existence, offers a good possibility to actualise Don Bosco's choice of a preventive pedagogy, and thus also to bridge any contradiction between the two perspectives.[1]

The triad 'kindness, reason, religion' goes back to Don Bosco himself. Sometimes he speaks of 'reason, kindness and religion' or 'reason, religion

1 For an initial elaboration, see: R. Burggraeve, 'Three-Dimensional Christian Values Education: Emotionality, Rationality and the Creation of Meaning', in: *Kristu Jyoti. A Youth Pastoral, Theological and Catechetical Quarterly* (Bangalore, India), Part I: 18 (2002) 1, March, 1–34; Part II: 18 (2002) 2, June 2002, 125–158. The present thorough reworking and further elaboration makes grateful use of two contributions at the Salesian Forum: (1) "Reason and Reasonableness as Pillars of Education. An Ethical Updating of Don Bosco's Legacy" (Valdocco-Torino, 2013); (2) "The Soul of Integral Education. Orientations for a contemporary interpretation of 'religione' in the Salesian pedagogical project" (Benediktbeuern, 2016). See also: R. Burggraeve, *Meerstemmig opvoeden*, (Antwerpen: Halewijn, 2015), 9–56: 'Deel I. Opvoeden met hart en ziel. Vrijmoedig in gesprek met Don Bosco'.

and kindness'. Sometimes he mentions only two pillars: 'reason and religion' or 'reason and kindness'. The order of the concepts and the content of their interpretation tend to vary from time to time.[2] We prefer to work with the triad in a distinct order: 'kindness, reason, religion'. Why we choose this option will become clear in the course of our reflection on and interpretation of this trio. It will also become clear how the three terms are not isolated but interconnected and dynamically interact with each other.[3]

Moreover, we approach this triad primarily as the foundation of education and therefore as a form of pedagogical spirituality. Don Bosco and his associates regularly qualify the two or three words as means and instruments, which puts the emphasis instead on the educational approach and style. Sometimes they speak of fundamental principles or pillars and driving forces, thus focusing on the foundation of education. We adhere to the latter approach without disregarding the fact that methodological aspects also flow from the triad. However, we see in the three words above all a framework and global orientation for the pedagogical practice, which also implies the inspiration for an individual existential way of living and acting, i.e., a Salesian lifestyle.

---

2 R. Biesmans, *Redelijkheid in de omgang met jongeren (1876–1884)* Don Bosco Studies n. 14, (Sint-Pieters-Woluwe: Don Bosco Centrale, 2000), 21–32.

3 R. Biesmans, *Amorevolezza*, Don Bosco Studies n. 15, (Sint-Pieters-Woluwe: Don Bosco Centrale, 2003), 23–24.

1. '*Amorevolezza*'

Warm-hearted Education[1]

We want to start our reflection on the pedagogical relationship in the spirit of Don Bosco with '*amorevolezza*' or 'kindness'. The educational relationship is a complex event. It involves an interaction between the educator[2] and the educatee (*educandus*),[3] namely the child or growing young person. It always takes place in an objective educational context such as a family, a school, youth association, 'oratorio', playground, shelter or other facility. In short, some kind of educational environment, mostly organised but sometimes rather informal or accidental.

1 We understand 'education' in a broad sense, namely as upbringing, and should therefore not be reduced to the traditional understanding of education as instruction or school.

2 We use the term 'educator' in a gender-neutral sense, in that it refers to the relationship of any educator, male or female, with any educatee, male or female.

3 The Latin *educandus* literally means: the person to whom the work of education by the educator is intended, literally the 'educatee'. We use the term *educandus* to refer both to the child and the young person as the object of the pedagogical relationship. Note, however, that by stating that the child and the young person count as an 'object' of education does not mean that they would only be the 'direct object' or, put more eloquently, the 'addressees'. They are equally the 'subject' of their own education. Not only are they the ones for whom education takes place, they likewise take part as followers and protagonists in the education process. This is precisely why we speak of pedagogical relationship. In the full sense of the word, this is only possible between equal subjects, without dismissing their mutual differences.

Starting our reflection on the pedagogical relationship with *amorevolezza* is not something we do without hesitation, especially in the current context of the severe crisis caused by the paedophilia scandal in the Church (and society). Suspicion has arisen against the sensitive expression of pedagogical love. Some even wonder if the Salesian emphasis on 'making your love tangible', as we read it in Don Bosco's well-known 'Letter from Rome' May 10, 1884,[4] does not foster an anti-emancipatory paternalism that could provide a context for or possibly trigger all kinds of boundary violations, including sexual abuse. In the wake of this suspicion, one then makes a strong and justified plea for zero tolerance towards all violations and forms of abuse of power (cf. infra). There is a risk of going so far that attention to the emotion or the heart is lost: 'much law and little emotion'. From the understanding that affectivity and affection are the basis of all human relationships, we nevertheless choose to begin with the *amorevolezza* without masking the risk attached to any pedagogical love. The dynamic of desire that essentially draws affectivity forms the condition, context and matrix for all law and 'reason' as the second pillar in the pedagogical triad. That is why Don Bosco's fundamental option for tangible and reasonable love in his 'Letter from Rome' remains entirely valid. Last but not least, this primacy of tangible and sensitive love is confirmed by the anchoring of that pedagogical love in the alpha and omega of God's unconditional love, as will become clear in the third section on 'religion' as the soul and inspiration of integral education according to Don Bosco.

1.1. Educational Emotion and Affection

If we look up the writings by and about Don Bosco and the so-called 'preventive system', one immediately notices how the word *amorevolezza*[5] brings with it a cluster of related words expressing how 'effective' love becomes 'affective' love, which is visible and tangible. As Don Bosco describes it in his 'Letter from Rome': "The children (young people) must not only be loved, they must also be able to feel and realise it". Moreover, the word *amorevolezza* expresses

4 Cf. R. Biesmans, *De Magna Charta van het salesiaanse opvoedingssysteem. Hulpboekje*, Don Bosco Studies n. 18, (Sint-Pieters-Woluwe, Don Bosco Centrale), 2010.

5 Although '*amorevolezza*' was not the predominant term with Don Bosco, we prefer it from the later tradition, arguing that it is a container term that does contain the terms more frequently used by Don Bosco, such as gentleness (*dolcezza*) and meekness (*mansuetudine*) and the other concepts cited.

that it is not about the great, sublime and spiritual love with a capital letter, but about an affective love in everyday life that expresses itself effectively through all kinds of small expressions, words, attentions, gestures and actions.

As a result, the term '*amorevolezza*' becomes a *Gestalt*, a set of stylistic features that are intertwined and mutually evocative: cordiality, joviality, gentleness, kindness, affability, courteous and empathic manners. All of these stylistic features are intended to create an atmosphere of accessibility and trust between educator and *educatee*. Don Bosco also likes to use the term '*famigliarità*', which stands for casualness and uncomplicatedness in interpersonal interaction.[6] It presupposes the presence of the educators with the children or young people, which includes supervision, an aspect of 'reason' (cf. infra). That presence or '*assistenza*' is the opposite of aloofness and remote supervision from a guarded height. It relies on a certain directness in its dealings, which does not present itself as authoritarian, but precisely divests itself of its pedagogical position of power in order to be close to children and young people in an 'ordinary', that is spontaneous and informal, way, without having to sacrifice honesty and transparency and even firmness in its dealings. Even at difficult moments, for example in the context of adversarial or aggressive behaviour on the part of the educatee, the pedagogical dealings must not be purely functional or formal, but the educator must still try to approach the child or adolescent in an empathetic, compassionate and friendly manner. "The educator must try to make himself loved if he is to inspire respect and awe" (Don Bosco in his '*Il sistema preventivo*'). In other words, it concerns a moral authority based on love, or rather on sensitive love, of which 'reasonableness' in the pedagogical relationship is also an expression (more on this in the second part). This sensitive love can be called the 'subjective affectivity' in the sense that it is found and realised on the interpersonal experience level.

This amicable interaction requires a pedagogical climate that is 'familial'—which is not the same as 'familiar', as will be explained further. In the spirit of Don Bosco, we call this familial climate 'family spirit'. It implies the creation of an environment that offers security, through which children and young people can feel at home and 'come to terms'. This familial climate consists, of course, of the already mentioned affable manners between educator and

---

6 The term '*famigliarità*', along with 'trust', recurs as a refrain in Don Bosco's 'Letter from Rome'. Cf. R. Biesmans, *De Magna Charta van het salesiaanse opvoedingssysteem. Hulpboekje*, 7, 21, 22, 27,29.

educatee. However, it also consists of the amiable and gentle interaction among children and young people themselves. It is clear that this reciprocal positive treatment also implies forms of benevolence and politeness, which allows one to interact with each other in a dignified manner. In the second part of our contribution, it will become clear how this simultaneously amiable and dignified reciprocal interaction also implies respect for certain agreements and boundaries—for example, the prohibition of brutality and bullying. In other words, educating in and to family spirit implies paying explicit attention to group formation. In this way, children and young people can experience that they belong somewhere, that they are surrounded by other people through which they can experience connection and can also help build that connection themselves.

This emotional and affective embedding can we call, inspired by the American psychologist Donald W. Winnicott (1896–1971), the necessary 'potential space'. Education is, in the first place, creating an environment of safety and security, so that children and young people, both in themselves and in others, find an environment through which connections and attachments can develop, and through which one can also 'go out', that is, leave the safe nest and enter the outside world with its strangeness and newness. Only those who have a home can, literally, go out, because then there is a difference between inside and outside, only then can one come back home from outside. There are young people who actually live outside and on the street and thus can never go out, precisely because they have no '*chez-soi*' or home to retreat to. Children and young people do not need big, abstract love, but the presence of people who create an atmosphere of warm, careful and sensitive cordiality. This well-felt affection takes place not only in interpersonal and group interaction but also extends to the material forms of the spaces where people are together and live. Hence the importance of the atmospheric design and cosy decoration of spaces that make tangible the commonality of being together and belonging. We can also call it the 'objective affectivity', in the sense that the environment of a home or living space itself creates the opportunities for reciprocal interaction between educator and educatee and between children and/or young people themselves.

1.2. A "Good Enough Mother"

However, the plea for emotionality and affectivity as the basis for education is not without risks. After all, psychoanalytically translated, this means the return to the mother or the maternal dimension, risking a relapse into 'fusion', this is the reductive fusion through which the distinction between 'mother' and 'child', between educator and educatee, is lost, with all the pernicious consequences that this entails. Particularly in the period of processing the past, recently surfaced and also current possible sexual abuse, a thorough critical reflection on the pedagogical affection of the '*amorevolezza*' is not a luxury.[7] In this context, Winnicott offers an important educational perspective with his idea of a "good enough mother".[8] Educators always embody the symbolic standing of the maternal figure. At the same time, they face the challenge of being only sufficiently good and not totally good 'mothers'. Neither the educational environment, the group nor the educator should be a 'perfect mother'. Then everything would run perfectly, then there would only be complete reciprocity, mutuality and involvement, without frustrations, deficits and crises. Such a perfect, rounded concept aligns with the child's desire to seek from other adults, especially educators, an extension of the original enclosing and embracing mother's womb. But also growing young people, who are trying to break free and emancipate themselves from the emotional entanglement of home, are looking for new forms of support and security. However, even though in their emotional chaos they need a 'substitute mother', this cannot be a double of their first mother that nurtured them. They need an environment and companions or educators who will give them a new sense of security, but without imprisoning or suffocating them. Their new environment and companions must therefore avoid all affective intrusiveness and confiscation. Young people, but also children, need an emotional closeness that uses the necessary caution and restraint.

It is precisely this kind of reserved, warm-hearted love that does not tie children and particularly young people to their educators or supervisors but,

---

7 X. Thévenot, 'Don Bosco éducateur et le "système préventif". Un examen mené à partir de l'anthropologie psychanalytique', in: ID., *Compter sur Dieu. Études de théologie morale*, (Paris: Cerf, 1992), 211–254, namely 238–248: "La place de l'amorevolezza et de l'amour".

8 D.W. Winnicott, *The Child, the Family and the Outside World*, (London: Penguin Books, 1973), 10, 173; B. Thomas, *A Good Enough Mother*, (London: Faber & Faber, 2020).

on the contrary, directs them to their peers in order to further develop their emotional and relational life. Education consists precisely in creating the potential space to develop 'horizontal or symmetric relations' in a healthy and qualitative way, i.e., relations with people of the same age, where the emphasis lies on the relationship with like-minded people of similar age. Group unions, camaraderie and friendships are, not only for children but also and especially for adolescents, predominantly the school of love, this is of trust, loyalty, honesty.

1.3. 'Non-incestuous' or 'Chaste' (Educational) Relationships

Continuing the idea of the 'good enough mother', we want to make a plea here for 'chaste' educational (and non-educational) relationships, based on a recalibration of the old (and outdated) concept of 'chastity'. For this actualising recalibration, we appeal to the prohibition of incest, which, in the wake of Xavier Thévenot (1938–2004),[9] Salesian of Don Bosco and moral theologian, we in turn give an expanded meaning. Precisely by linking chastity with the prohibition against incest, he broadens the strict sexual significance of chastity into a general human significance (in which, of course, the sexual significance is included).

The incest prohibition, namely that no sexual contact may take place between parents and children nor between members of the same family or one's own relatives, functions as the foundation of civilisation precisely because it draws an unassailable boundary between the generations. By broadening this strict significance of the incest prohibition in relational terms, however, we end up in a recalibration of 'chastity' as 'non-incestuous'. To make this clear, Thévenot starts with the etymology of the word 'chastity', which remarkably enough is laden with a deep anthropological—generally human—truth. The word 'chaste' in fact goes back to the Latin '*castus*'. The opposite of '*castus*' is '*incastus*', of which '*incestus*' is a synonym and is translated as 'incestuous'. In other words, in terms of etymology, one who is incestuous is unchaste. This etymological remark, however, is only interesting when one interprets

---

9 X. Thévenot, *Repères éthiques pour un monde nouveau*, (Mulhouse: Salvator, 1982), 44–52; ID., *Les péchés: que peut-on en dire?* (Mulhouse: Salvator, 1993), 29–31.

the term 'incestuous' more broadly than the common linguistic usage where, as we already mentioned, a sexual relationship with a next of kin is meant. In the perspective of this broadening, we consider as incest every behaviour that strives to extend and to repeat the indistinguishable state that exists at the beginning of life between child and mother. A behaviour is then chaste when one is made capable of surpassing the condition of amalgamation and fusion at the beginning of one's existence.

For this, we find a link in the field of psychoanalysis. It points out that for a child, learning to live in a human manner means acquiring its 'separateness and independence', whereby it opens up to those other than itself, learning to develop a respectful relationship with others. This is only possible by breaking away from 'immersed participation', by separating itself gradually from the fusing oneness (in psychology: fusional)—the bondedness—with her or his origin, in other words by differentiating oneself. Or put differently, by definitively losing and abandoning her or his origin. We can paraphrase here the Gospel text: "For those who want to save their life will lose it, and those who lose their life for my sake will find it" (Matt 16:25), by saying: "For those who want to save their fusional lives will lose their human lives, and those who lose their fusional (immersed and amalgamated) lives for the sake of those other than oneself will save their human lives." We must abandon literally and figuratively, factually and emotionally, our mother's bosom, the parental nest, to be able to bond with those other than ourselves in a non-consuming, liberating manner.

It turns out here how human life and growth always implies a 'renunciation', namely a renunciation of the undifferentiated and fused condition of coinciding with one's own origin. The seductive charm of this identification manifests itself very clearly on a relational level, in that one experiences the other as the salvaging, encompassing, and nurturing mother figure, through which one is also total and perfect and omnipotent: the 'heaven on earth', where one is totally at home with oneself by being totally at home with others. One dreams of a world without difference, which easily leads—almost without one noticing it—to the incestuous and therefore unchaste dissolution of otherness. Think, for example, of certain youth groups, which are completely horizontal: one lets oneself be absorbed in mood music, drinking, being sociable with each other as friends and equals, without any form of authority or law, absorbed in the mutual chatter without disagreements, without disorders and difficulties from outside... timelessly and wordlessly intertwined, without gaps and conflicts. Therefore, a community or a group can be unchaste, namely when it practises and experiences the 'myth' of total transparency and closeness, of total compassion and availability. This myth, or ideology, reflects the dream of absolute, horizontal reciprocity, which consequently tolerates neither privacy nor unbalanced power relations. Only forms of direct proximity are accepted, while all mediations via agreements and rules, symbols and rituals or fixed habits, or via the 'givenness' of an institutional setting, are rejected as inconvenient and conservative. People want to meet and deal with each other directly, without having to go through the diversions of objective figures, rules and structures. Such a community experience seems 'fantastic' at first glance, but on closer inspection, it is a magically inflated 'fantasy' and imagination which, moreover, leads to violence. Similarly, the removed difference between friends or lovers is unchaste, or certainly becomes unchaste if, after the initial flame of the 'click' or the infatuation, it is perpetuated and absolutised into 'real' love or the only 'real' friendship: 'We share everything together!'—'We do everything together!'—'What you want, I want too!'—'We are an open book to each other: no secrets between us!' Or, as once heard on a train from a young couple who were completely entwined whispering to each other, "You're perfect! I'm perfect! It's perfect!" When this becomes the basis for a relationship, it involuntarily becomes so suffocating that the connection for the future is replaced by the intensity in the here and now: literally an eternal 'now' moment that must last! A form of incestuous unchastity which sooner or later separates the partners!

How the risk of incestuous unchastity is inherent in any close relationship, and how awareness of this risk can lead to a non-incestuous, chaste relationship, is eloquently expressed by the well-known psychoanalyst Françoise Dolto at the age of nine in a short letter (Sunday, August 3, 1916) to her mother during her stay with her grandmother, with whom she has a very close relationship. Not from her *'chez-soi'*, (first home) but from that 'other' house, the *'chez-soi'* at her grandmother's, she writes a letter to her mother telling her anecdotally what is happening there and how well she is doing. At the end of that letter is a phrase that also expresses her warm relationship with her mother. Apparently, it is best to appreciate the warmth of home when one is not at home, when one is elsewhere! Françoise writes in poor French, "*Je t'embrasse très, très, très fort*"—"I embrace you very, very, very strongly". Without affectively affirming attachment, one cannot live! But immediately she adds, "*mais pas à te casser la figure*"—"but without crushing your face".[10] Little Françoise apparently already realises that such a strong embrace in which one presses all the way against the other can lead to a squeezing, unchaste, embrace where one can be so absorbed in each other that one crushes each other. A bit like lovers sometimes say, 'I love you so much, I would like to eat you': then one becomes part of the other, which can be called a form of cannibalism, and thus—on reflection—an intolerable form of incest and unchastity. Even though at first glance it seems like a very romantic idea, namely that one loves the other so much that one becomes completely one with the other, this unification happens by consuming the other. Even if this assimilation happens with mutual consent, it remains a form of reduction of the one to the other, and consequently of violence. A chaste love renounces 'eating' the other or allowing itself to 'be eaten' by the other, so a non-incestuous coupling unity can emerge.

From this, it appears that no human being is born chaste, but that one becomes chaste, aided precisely to this end by the crisis caused by the prohibition[11] of coexisting with one's own origin. Chastity is no self-evident fact but a task, and it is not given once but time and time again. One is not chaste; one *becomes* chaste. And this happens precisely through a humanising interaction with one's own desires in confrontation with reality. In that confrontation, one learns to renounce the world without difference and without inadequacy, and a world of omnipotence where one would be the central point as an absolute master. And note well, this is not only applicable to the mother-child relationship, but to all later relationships. It is namely in the relationships with new, non-maternal others that every human is faced time and again with the temptation to repeat or to 'demand' the original fusional connectedness with the mother, whereby the new relationships in turn become again incestuous and thus unchaste. Hence the challenge that appears not once but time and time again is to renounce the, at times, strong, passionate temptation of fusional relationships.

This is especially true for adolescents who often have rather romantic notions about intimate love, and who easily confuse intensity with sustainability.

---

10 F. Dolto, *Correspondance 1913–1938*, edited by Colette Percheminier, Jean 'Carlos' Dolto, Grégoire Dolto, Catherine Dolto-Tolitich, (Paris: Hatier, 1991), 67.

11 Here already emerges a vital aspect of 'reason', namely the indispensable role of 'law'. This will be developed more systematically in the second part of this essay.

In the development of their adolescence, they are looking for a unique other who is more than a comrade, that is, someone who for them has all the characteristics of a friend. They crave someone with whom they have a privileged relationship. Only when you are someone's chosen one do you feel appreciated. In addition, they no longer feel alone or one of the many, a number in the grey mass. In this way they feel special, not only in the eyes of that one other person, but also in the eyes of the others, their classmates and peers. They also like to be seen by these others together, because in this way the appreciation—or envy—of these others returns to them. In other words, this is how they build their self-esteem.[12] In line with this emerges the romantic dream of a great love. And the more deeply felt and physical that love is, the more they believe it is 'real' love: intensity-in-the-here-and-now through identification wins out over permanence, which is tested over time and through all kinds of differences.

For the pedagogical relationship, this means that it is only chaste when it is non-incestuous, that is, not fusional and confining but creating room for the independence and individuality (alterity) of the child or the young person. An educator should never give in to the desire for fusion, whether it shows up on his side or on the side of the educatee. A pedagogical relationship that is worthy of the name is faced with the appeal and the challenge to build up an asymmetrical reciprocity, so that the child or the young person would never be caught in and by the relationship. When Don Bosco suggests that the educator must be the 'friend' of the educatee, this then should not be understood wrongly, namely that the pedagogical relationship must take place as a reciprocal relationship between equals. The inequality and the level difference between educator (adult) and educatee (child, young person) need to be maintained and given a positive form. Otherwise, both the independence and freedom of the child or young person are compromised as well as their possibility of establishing contacts and building up relationships with new others outside of the pedagogical relationship. A pedagogical relationship is only chaste when it respects and promotes asymmetry and difference. This also explains why Don Bosco immediately links the qualification of the educator as friend with that of father: 'friend and father'. Through his pedagogical task, he is invested with the authority and responsibility to lead the minor, which

---

12 F. Sand and Y. de Gentil-Baichis (eds.), *Le couple au risque de la durée*, (Paris: Desclée de Brouwer, 1998), particularly 51–65: '4. Le parcours des bébés-couples'.

goes beyond all simple and simplistic symmetry. Abolishing pedagogical asymmetry creates a fertile environment for the abuse of power, including emotional intimidation and sexual abuse, as well as forms of unhealthy confidentiality and familiarity.[13] Hence, in line with the cautious Salesian tradition, 'particular' or 'tender friendships' are unacceptable, including their physical expressions—like touching the face, hugging the educatee, being embraced by the educatee—precisely because they easily become ambiguous and pave the way for infringing the integrity and intimacy of children or young people.[14] In our interaction and proximity, the necessary distance must always be preserved: it is about a cautious and careful interaction, a true proximity without captivating the child or young person and generating their dependence on us.[15]

We can also describe it as a proximity that is accompanied by shuddering or '*frikè*', the Greek word with which Plato also qualifies the noble *eros* (love and desire): emotional and physical shivering at the same time. In the desire to be close to the other, by virtue of the attraction there is hesitation in the approach.[16] As a dynamic event, proximity is a form of caution and restraint. In coming close, one does not want to take possession of the other. One recedes and becomes tender and caring for the sake of the other's otherness, which is at the same time strong and vulnerable. In my approach to the other, I realise that I must not force the other. Thus, proximity as 'approach' expresses the ethical appeal—the *frikè* or emotion of shivering—not to be reductive, nor devouring or tyrannising, not to affect the other and lock her or him up in dependence. One approaches the other with timidity. Timidity as a fear of profaning or harming the other. Yet a love that comes near. A love that is both patient and 'slow'! Only an 'affirmative and sensitive love with shivering'

13 R. Biesmans, *Amorevolezza*, 196–205.

14 Already in the decisions of the first General Chapter (19877) of the Salesian Congregation these expressions are "strictly forbidden" (cited by R. Biesmans, *Amorevolezza*, 204). This strict position should make it possible to fully incarnate the pedagogical style of benevolent friendliness and 'familiarity' in the positive sense: to be close to children and young people in such a way that they can talk about their home life, about what moves them, as they would in a casual and friendly interaction in the family. See: R. Biesmans, *Amorevolezza*, 189–196.

15 Cf. C. Loots, *Offensori e vittime faccia a faccia: mediazione nel contesto di abusi sessuali*, Forum Salesiano, Munich (August 25–28, 2020).

16 E. Levinas, *Otherwise than Being of Beyond Essence*, Tr. A. Lingis, (The Hague/Boston/London: Martinus Nijhoff Publishers, 1981), 84, 87, 185, 192.

is non-suffocating and consequently pedagogically responsible. Only in that way, thanks to the educational relationship, can the gradual emotional maturity of children and young people grow.[17]

---

17 Cf. A.A.A. Terruwe, *Grondbeginselen van levenskunst*, (Roermond: Romen, 1968); ID., *De frustratieneurose*, (Roermond: Romen, 1972); ID., *Mens-geworden zijn en bevestiging*, (Lochem: De Tijdstroom, 1973); ID., *Geef mij je hand*, (Lochem: De Tijdstroom, 1978).

2. *'Ragione'*

Reasonable Education

By linking *amorevolezza* with chastity, we have also inadvertently linked it with the law as prohibition. With this, we would like to contrast with the previously discussed and current one-sidedness of 'much law and little emotion' a second contemporary one-sidedness under criticism: 'much emotion and little law'.[1] Emotion without law is out of control and lethal. In the previous section, we saw clearly how an external agency is needed to break through the desire for synthesis with one's own origin, with the intention of also adopting the perfect and absolute character of that origin, or rather to break open to the 'other than oneself', so that one can turn to new realities and also leave the immersed participation to go out into the world and have all kinds of new experiences there. That agency is the law, whose symbolic representative is the 'father', namely the 'reality principle' as Freud calls it, along which a human being must pass to become independent and free. In the idea of law we see, in contrast to emotion (*amorevolezza*), a figure of reason, the second dimension of the Salesian pedagogical triad: *ragione*. Pedagogical love, which always runs the all too human risk of fusing identification, must be guided in all its geniality, familiarity and closeness at the same time by the objectivity of reason.

---

1 T. Anatrella, *La différence interdite. Sexualité, éducation, violence trente ans après mai 1968*, (Paris: Flammarion, 1998).

Remarkably, Don Bosco and the Salesian tradition interchange two terms, namely reason (*ragione*) and reasonableness (*ragionevolezza*). Even though they are intertwined in reality, they still deserve to be distinguished from each other. While reasonableness is particularly about the style of pedagogical treatment, reason is rather involved with rationality as the surpassing of subjective emotion and thus as the confrontation with what is objectively true and valuable. Hence, before we reflect on reasonableness as a pedagogical method, we first anchor this reasonableness in an ethical reflection on law and prohibition.

2.1. No Humanising Education without Boundary Rules

A very distinctive and essential way in which the law presents itself is the moral or ethical law. It also played an important role with Don Bosco, inspired by his Christian faith. It is well known how he held quite strict moral standards and insights, influenced by his seminary education. And he was not averse to 'discipline' in the Oratorio in Turin, although at the same time it could be very cheerful and casual, especially during the moments of recreation.[2] In addition, in his basic text, 'The Preventive Method in the Education of Youth', he unequivocally emphasises the importance of reason through law and structure: "The preventive method consists in knowing and making known the regulations and rules of the [educational] institution".[3] He also thinks that educators, for fear of losing sympathy, should not be apprehensive of reprimanding their young people, as is evident from the 'Rules for the Houses', to which he and his close associates attached great importance, as is evident from the way in which it was worked on and also adjustments and amendments were discussed and introduced. With all this, Don Bosco rebalances the risk of the unbalanced affective attachment of the educatee to the educator. With an educator who makes demands, one can no longer totally identify. The law creates distance, or rather the necessary distance, so that reason enters into emotion.

2 G. Bosco, *Il sistema preventivo*, 85/445, quoted by R. Biesmans, *Redelijkheid in de omgang met jongeren (1876–1884)*, 74: "One must give ample opportunity to jump, to run, to make life to one's heart's content." Don Cafasso, his spiritual mentor, guarded Don Bosco from applying the (moral) law too rigorously in practice (cf. also infra).

3 Quoted by: X. Thévenot, 'Don Bosco éducateur et le "système préventif"', 234, note 33.

So when we speak of 'law', it is important to note immediately that we are not talking about rules arbitrarily promulgated by some accidental, factual body or authority, but about rules which are expressions of reason, or rather of universal reason, according to Immanuel Kant[4], that is, which exhibit a general human validity precisely because they attempt to express the humane. In moral theology, one speaks of the 'natural law' in this context, in that they are expressions of humanness (humanity) beyond all subjective and accidental circumstances.

Specifically, we want to make explicit the connection between reason and law on the basis of a thorough reflection on the creative meaning of the prohibition, not so much to be understood as the legal regulatory prohibition, namely the formal regulation in a group's organised life, but the ethical prohibition, which from now on will be simply referred to as prohibition. For that purpose, we take our starting point in the narrative of the so-called rich young man (Matt 19; Mk 10; Lk 18).

When a man, not a Pharisee or specialist in the Torah [the Law], but just 'someone', being wealthy, and—for Luke—also powerful and honoured, asked Jesus to show him the way to eternal and full life, he received as an answer: "If you wish to ENTER INTO [not STEP OUT OF] life, keep the commandments" (Matt 19:17b). Jesus refers that person to the second tablet of the Ten Commandments,[5] namely the prohibitions:[6] "not murder, not commit adultery, not steal, not bear false witness". The question then immediately arises and, in all seriousness, certainly today as we are more than attached to freedom and our own desires and preferences: how can prohibition and life go together? Are not prohibition and life simply irreconcilable, just as our spontaneous intuition suggests? For an answer to

4 See: G. Buchdahl, *Kant and the Dynamics of Reason: Essays on the Structure of Kant's Philosophy*, (Oxford: Blackwell, 1992).

5 See concerning the Ten Commandments: M.-A. Ouaknin, *Les dix commandements*, (Paris: Seuil, 1999). According to Israel Cohen, "Every education must renew the connection with the Ten Commandments." Quoted by: V. Malka, *Les mots de la sagesse juive*, (Paris: Desclée de Brouwer, 2012), 105.

6 Ibid., 105: "Every education begins with prohibitions" (Leo Baeck).

this question, we again take inspiration from the insights of Xavier Thévenot on the 'paradox of the prohibition'.[7]

At first sight, the prohibition seems completely negative but precisely in and through its negativity it offers more room for freedom and creativity than the commandment that prescribes an action. Indeed, a prohibition opens up the field of human possibilities because it only outlines the boundary of humaneness and does not determine nor indicate normatively that which is humane or meaningful.[8]

What is characteristic of the prohibition is that it appeals to human creativity by closing off the impasses and wrong tracks. A simple example in the field of education can make this clear. Imagine a family with children going for a walk in the forest. When they come upon an intersection with five paths the 'problem' arises as to which path the children (will) have to take. The parents can tackle this problem in two ways. One possibility is that they themselves determine which path is the best for the children, and they normatively impose this path. With this, they can act directly in an imperative and authoritative way, or—what usually happens—rather indirectly by cajoling and 'dressing up' the best path that they present to their children. They present this path in such a magnificent and enticing way, for instance by pointing out the largest circus—the wonderful reward—that awaits them at the end of the path and the colourful and fascinating attractions of various clowns, artists, acrobats and magicians along the way. As a result, not only the end-goal but also the path itself is presented pleasantly, in the hope that they can bring their children without coercion, as it were, to choose the 'best' path that is laid out for them. Such a values education, however, easily falls prey to ideological manipulation, even though it camouflages its authoritarian-imposing character behind the façade of a decorated and embellished positive value-attraction.[9] In this way, the freedom of the growing young person is greatly restricted, if not radically

---

7 X. Thévenot, *Souffrance, bonheur, éthique. Conférences spirituelles*, (2nd ed.), (Mulhouse: Salvator, 1990), 61–89.

8 P. Beauchamp, *D'une à l'autre montagne. La loi de Dieu*, (Paris: Seuil, 1969), 30–34.

9 In this regard, we would like to refer to a statement by Yeshayahu Leibowitz: "Education does not consist in transmitting values but in making man capable of appropriating them." Quoted by: V. Malka, *Les mots de la sagesse juive*, 105.

assailed and destroyed. The other possibility consists in that the parents only intervene educationally when their children are about to take one of the five paths that is a dead-end: "Do you not see what that sign says: 'No entry: dead-end road'?" By means of this approach the creativity of the educatees is not restrained, but on the contrary challenged, since four other paths are laid open among which they themselves must now choose. They can try out the remaining options for themselves and experience by trial and error which is the most satisfactory path for them. The prohibition does not say what they must do, what is best for them; it only says what they must not do in order to not end up in the wrong. The prohibition refers only to the other paths as possibilities by denying entrance to, or rather by prohibiting, the dead-end path. The prohibition possesses especially 'the virtue of the negative': it prevents children and young people from becoming mercenaries of the law, meaning to say slavish followers and executers of an instruction. It also arouses in them the necessary resistance against those that enact or perform the law, thereby guarding them from unthinkingly—overly enthusiastically—identifying with the educator, with all its risks of some form of abuse.

Refraining from the negative, a disvalue (e.g., bullying) meaning to say not committing a verbal violence, is in itself not yet a merit. Although this restraint is already an achievement and can call for much effort, everything else still remains to be done. In this regard, the prohibition opens up the path for creative freedom, which may give shape to the value protected and profiled by the prohibition according to its own insights and capacities. To use an image from football: prohibitions draw out only the lines on the football field within which a football match can be played. They only make the football match possible; of themselves, they are in no way the game itself. Even when there are perfect and indisputable game rules, of themselves they do not guarantee a high-quality football game. Even the referee does not offer any certainty for high-class football. He or she is only there to lead the game in the right direction and is only visible when an offence is committed. Only then does the referee intervene to prevent the football match from being affected as such, without being concerned further with the quality of the game. (The referee does not blow the whistle, for instance, to point out to the public the magnificent game of one of the players or of the entire team...) For a qualitative football game, more is needed, namely, good players who, under the leadership of a skilled coach, not only further develop their playing capacity but also form together a team with spirit and commitment.

In the same manner, prohibitions are like boundary rules that draw the lines within which human dignity can be developed, without themselves determining the content and quality of human dignity. In other words, by opening up the path to freedom, the prohibition opens up the path to personal, interpersonal and communal creativity giving shape according to one's own insight and capability to the value that is protected and profiled by the prohibition. The prohibition only points out a 'path of death' and for the rest leaves people with the full responsibility to discover and explore the 'path of life'.

Let us illustrate this paradoxical relationship between prohibition on the one hand and freedom and creativity on the other based on the already cited prohibitions from the second tablet of the Ten Commandments. Except for the prohibition against adultery, which in its particularity concerns intimate sexual relationships, the other prohibitions—do not kill, steal, bear false witness or lie—have a general application in the sense that they concern all possible relationships between people. We propose, therefore, for the purposes of our discourse, to understand the prohibition of adultery also in a general human sense as a prohibition of cheating and unfaithfulness: thou shalt not forsake another. If we try to positively formulate one of these prohibitions, a shift in levels always takes place. While the prohibition forbids a concrete, negative deed or action, for instance 'to kill', 'to lie', 'to steal', 'to cheat', where it turns out that a prohibition also implies a double denial, namely not do something negative, the corresponding commandment lends itself to be understood as the quality of the morality of the person, or as attitude and virtue. The positive reverse-side of 'You shall not kill' is the appeal to 'respect for life', of 'You shall not lie' the task to honesty and authenticity, of 'You shall not steal' the imperative to 'respect property (mine and thine)', and of 'Thou shalt not cheat', the imperative to loyalty and creative fidelity.

No quality of proximity, of caring and love between persons, is possible if killing takes place, just as no honest society based on trust and confidence, no respect for what is mine and thine nor loyalty and fidelity are possible if stealing, lying and cheating are committed. When aggressiveness, lying, disrespect for 'mine and thine' and cheating become fundamental drives, i.e., when one starts from the principle that one in all circumstances and equally towards anyone may speak untruths, may violate the 'ownness' of others, may use violence, betray and cheat, a humane social life is fundamentally undermined. But with that, all is not yet said about ethics. For if people do not use violence against each other, there still is no concrete experience of love and caring. Or when people do not lie to each other, an atmosphere of trust and authenticity is not automatically created. Or if people don't cheat on each other or let each other down, that doesn't mean that there is automatically an atmosphere of loyalty and fidelity. Just as there is not yet respect for what is mine and thine, nor recognition of each other's uniqueness and contribution in a relationship or in a community when people do not steal from each other or do not violate the uniqueness of the other. When one observes the prohibitions and does not commit violence, not lie or cheat, and not 'steal' what 'belongs' to the other, one has not yet done anything in order to realise a life-promoting, upright, respectful and faithful interhuman and social relation. Of course, the minimum prerequisites for that purpose are present. The space for humane and loving relationships is created. There is a bottom in the glass that is, however, not yet filled with water. The bottom is indeed necessary, or else everything is spilled away, but in that case the glass is not yet filled with drink. To fill the glass is not only not doing something, but also doing something tangible. But for this definitive act, namely the real authentication of non-violent, genuine, fair and loyal relationships, in which also people's differences are acknowledged and valued in discernible forms and signs, one cannot rely on the prohibition. For that, one must appeal entirely to the capacity of one's own freedom in order to creatively design the shapes and paths of effective respect for life, trust, respect for what is mine and thine, reliability and fidelity.

An important pedagogical aspect of this view on ethical prohibitions is that they are valid for both sides of the pedagogical relationship, namely not only for the educatee but also for the educator. The prohibitions, as we have drawn them from the narrative of the rich man and the second tablet of the Ten Commandments, represent the outlines of the pedagogical playing field in the sense that the educators are oriented in their educative treatment of children and young people by the prohibition against violence, theft (annulling difference), lying, cheating and infidelity, because only in this way does the educative relationship acquire a frame that is worthy of human dignity. This dimension deserves our time, with its special attention to the 'victims' of all sorts of violence and abuse (cf. supra). On the other hand, as boundary rules the prohibitions are also applicable to the behaviour of the educatee. An essential goal of education is indeed that children and young people are initiated into the symbolic order—the playing field—of human values and norms via the prohibitions. As boundary rules they trace the conditions for the protection, acknowledgement and development of their own personal unassailability and integrity as well as those of others ('you shall not kill'). They also create space for authentic relationships ('you shall not lie/ not bear false witness') that at the same time command respect for each other's individuality and difference ('you shall not steal') and establish reciprocal fidelity and loyalty ('you shall not cheat').

All of this can be summarised as follows: the prohibitions form the "basic conditions for love"[10] without filling it in, without determining and prescribing how this love should be concretely shaped. In this respect the prohibitions are only the first and necessary stage on the way to love in freedom: "only the beginning of freedom, not perfect freedom".[11] We can also call them the riverbed, which through its banks embeds love. If the river were to step outside its banks, it could cause great damage and destruction, or it could become a swamp in which one sinks. If the water remains within its banks, the river winds through the landscape with all its hills and valleys, moorings and vistas. As banks embedding the flowing water, they also help direct the course of the river, without, however, being the source and force and mouth of the flowing river.

2.2. Pedagogical Reasonableness

This initiation of children and young people is a learning process, marked by trial and error, progress and regress, and in any case by a versatile and wrinkle-free dynamism. Humane behaviour does not fall out of the sky nor is innate but is the result of a gradual discovery and practice, which exactly demonstrates the necessity of education.

For this we find inspiration in the so-called 'law of gradualness', as it was launched and introduced by John Paul II in the apostolic exhortation on the

---

10 In his encyclical *Veritatis Splendor* (1983) John Paul II, inspired by Augustine, labels the prohibitions of the second tablet as "the basic condition for love of neighbour", John Paul II, *Veritatis Splendor*, (St Peter's Basilica, Vatican City, August 6, 1993), n. 13.

11 Ibid.

family '*Familiaris Consortio*',[12] and reaffirmed and developed by Francis I in the post-synodal exhortation '*Amoris Laetitia*'.[13] This documents interpret the 'law of gradualness' (*FC* 34; *AL* 293–295) as the "dynamic process" (*FC* 9) of the step by step and unceasing progress of people in their moral life to "advance gradually with the progressive integration of the gifts of God and the demands of God's definitive and absolute love in their entire personal and social life" (*AL* 295). The concept of gradualness rests on the conviction that the human person is a historical being: "But man, who has been called to live God's wise and loving design in a responsible manner, is a historical being who day by day builds himself up through his many free decisions; and so he knows, loves and accomplishes moral good by stages of growth" (*FC* 34). The psychological sciences have familiarised us with the development of the person, both on bodily, psychological and affective levels, as well as on moral and spiritual levels. This leads to the insight that gradualness, however, does not stand on its own since it concerns an orientated growth. This growth cannot take place in the wild; it must be directed at a goal, namely the realisation of meaningful living and acting, in the Christian sense a meaningful loving.[14]

Such an 'ethics of growth', namely the gradual (existential) learning and development precisely demonstrates the necessity of education: "an educating growth process is necessary" (*FC* 9). At the same time, we arrive at the second significance of reason, namely 'reasonableness'.[15] The initiation in the world

12 John Paul II, *Familiaris Consortio*, (St Peter's Basilica, Vatican City, November 22, 1981) [*FC*].

13 Francis, *Amoris Laetitia*, (St Peter's Basilica, Vatican City, March 19, 2016) [*AL*].

14 Cf. R. Burggraeve, *On the Way to Sustainable Love. Ethical Stepping Stones for a Christian and Salesian Relational and Sexual Education of Growth in a Pluralist Society [in the Light of Pope Francis' Logic of Mercy and Discernment (Amoris Laetitia)]*, Forum Salesiano 2018, Wien, Available: http://www.salesian.online/wp-content/uploads/2021/01/2018-08-23-8-Roger-Burggraeve-On-the-way-to-sustainable-love.pdf [Accessed 08/06/2022]; ID., 'Invoking the hidden resilience of vulnerable love. The Fundamental Aspects for an Ethics of Growth in the Light of Pope Francis' "Logic of Pastoral Mercy and Discernment" in Amoris Laetitia', in *Asian Horizons*, 12 (2018), No. 2, June, 247–261.

15 Cf. C. Nanni, *Ragione e ragionevolezza ai tempi di Don Bosco… e oggi?* (Salesian Forum, Turin, 2013), 11 pp. Available: http://www.salesian.online/wp-content/uploads/2020/12/2013-08-28-Carlo-Nanni-Ragione-e-ragionevolezza.pdf [Accessed 08/06/2022].

of law and reason takes place—says Don Bosco—according to a particular pedagogical style, namely the '*ragionevolezza*',[16] to be understood as a form of 'practical wisdom' in the line of Aristotle's virtue of '*phronèsis*' (prudence).[17] Here he also attempts to offer an alternative to the so-called repressive system that, on the basis of the depravity of humans, proceeds from the assumption that education takes place through strict discipline[18] and that wanton behaviour and the violation of regulations must be corrected unrelentingly (cf. today's increasing call for 'zero tolerance' against and punishment of petty crime and nuisance by young people).

A humanising education cannot suffice with a subjective educational climate that is emotionally 'sheltering', but at the same time has need for explanation and confrontation, i.e., a form of objectivity. Education should not only be emotional but also rational, meaning reasonable and therefore discursive and argumentative. If education would only happen by means of an immersion in the emotionality of a 'cosy home base', in which one enjoyably participates for consolation and comfort, then one ends up in the risk of manipulation that makes use of affectivity in order to lure (especially vulnerable) children or growing young people into too much dependence and, at times, even to a form of invisible slavery. Nonetheless, it is precisely the right significance and task of becoming adult that one no longer lets oneself be determined by another than oneself ('*Fremdbestimmung*' 'heteronomy') but determines oneself by oneself ('*Selbstbestimmung*' 'self-determination'), both in responsibility for oneself as well as for others. That is why every education should grow towards an honest and objective confrontation with that which is worthwhile, and this by means of reasoning and discussion, because these create the objectivity and necessary distance whereby one no longer feels emotionally owned but is

16 Cf. R. Biesmans, *Redelijkheid in de omgang met jongeren (1876–1884)*, 141pp.

17 Cf. M. Pellerey, *Educare alla ragione e con la ragione nel contesto del sistema educativo salesiano: verso un principio di ragionevolezza pedagogica* (Salesian Forum 2013), 15 pp. Available: http://www.salesian.online/wp-content/uploads/2020/12/2013-08-28-4-Michele-Pellerey-Educare-alla-ragione-e-con-la-ragione.pdf [Accessed 08/06/2022].

18 Cf. the whitewashing in the past of maltreatment in boarding schools, orphanages and facilities of special child welfare that now rise to the surface thanks to the testimonies of 'victims' who never have been able to work out what was inflicted on them and who at first never could or dared to come out in the open with their stories.

enabled to think and to judge for oneself, and gradually to arrive at one's own views. On the other hand, it is only in the context of sheltering emotionality that the element of rationality can be constructively introduced, because rationality and its 'rules' (law) with all its frustrations are too hard and hurtful without the embedding in emotionality, surely for the educatee—the child or the young person—who is just leaving the nest.[19]

First, in the Salesian pedagogy this means that special attention should be paid to reasonableness with which agreements and regulations are drawn up and communicated or discussed and developed in consultation with the children and young people, according to their level of development. Don Bosco found the appeal to healthy common sense indispensable, whereby all pretentious insincerity and authoritarian exercise of power in the interaction between educators and children or young people need to be avoided. Educators must have the courage and the humility to likewise appeal to the intelligence of the educatee. This presupposes honest and clear communication with reliable information on what is necessary and expected in order to make the educative environment function in a liveable and healthy and 'familial' manner. One should not forget that it usually does not suffice to provide information on agreements and *modi operandi* only once, and that one should repeat the matter regularly. Time and time again, it is important not only to repeat the agreement but also to provide a motivation for it, and if necessary, to adjust and justify it more correctly in line with changing circumstances. By so doing, a reasonable education remains a dynamic process that also takes a critical stance towards oneself and thus avoids becoming rigid or degenerating into a, at times covert, 'totalitarian regime' or a 'back-breaking armour': "no coercive measures but persuasion" (Don Bosco). We can also call this the 'wisdom of love'.

Another important aspect in reasonableness as a pedagogical style and method is impartiality. Children and young people simply deserve equal treatment on the basis of their equality as human beings. Every child, every young person has the right to the same loving treatment and discursive dialogue. Every child and every young person deserve opportunities, and that is precisely what the pedagogical environment must help to create. Preferential treatment arouses disgruntlement and frustration precisely because one's deeply rooted sense

19 For the treatment of pedagogical reasonableness, we draw inspiration from: R. Biesmans, *Redelijkheid in de omgang met jongeren*, especially 35–53.

of justice is violated. If educators tackle the faults of the one more strictly than the others, then they themselves cause the disgruntlement—which, in turn, may tempt them to take hard or subtly repressive measures whereby the disgruntlement in the child or the young person only increases and, consequently, the pedagogical climate itself is affected. This impartiality should not, however, lead to neutrality in such a way that there is no longer any involvement or *amorevolezza*. Hence in this context we suggest making use of an idea of Ivan Boszormenyi-Nagy, namely 'multiple partiality'.[20] Indeed in their mutual, fundamental equality as humans and also as inimitable beings, with their own personality and story, people deserve to be treated as unique and as equals. Hence educators, precisely on the basis of the choice for *amorevolezza*, are called to bring all their attention and 'presence' for the individuality of children and young people. This is the only way they get the acknowledgement they deserve whereby they can become what they are: unique persons. This attention to or partiality for the uniqueness of the other should not lead, however, to exclusivism, preferential treatment and favouritism. That is precisely why multiple partiality is needed, in the sense that while listening to the story of one child, we try to let the stories of the other children resound in the story of the one child so that the unique child in question does not end up enclosed in its own narrow-minded perspective. At the same time, multiple partiality means that in our partiality for one child or young person, we remain equally partial to the other children or young people in the group or educational setting. If, for instance, tension or conflict arises between young people in a class or peer group, multiple partiality consists in listening to both (or all) parties of the conflict, taking on board their emotions and arguments, and on the basis of this multilateral attention stimulating a conversation and compromise between the parties. In that way, multiple partiality becomes an expression of Salesian reasonableness.

2.3. Restraint in Sanctioning

A third important aspect of Salesian pedagogical reasonableness is the way in which we deal with violations or transgressions and sanctions. On the one hand, determination is needed to retain certain agreements and boundary rules as expressions of important values, and this precisely to guarantee an

20 I. Boszormenyi-Nagy & B.R. Krasner, *Between Give and Take: A Clinical Guide to Contextual Therapy*, (Abingdon, Oxfordshire, UK: Routledge, 1986).

ethically qualitative pedagogical environment. In his 'Letter from Rome', which deals primarily with pedagogical love and the ways to make it visible and tangible, Don Bosco speaks very clearly about 'immoral behaviour' that cannot be accepted. He even argues for "implacability",[21] in the sense that those in charge should not hesitate to remove young people from the home or educational community if they harshly and/or repeatedly violate essential boundary rules, as we have interpreted 'immoral behaviour' above.

At the same time, sufficient mercy, patience and compassion are also needed to ensure understanding for the mistakes and errors of children and young people without thereby explaining away what was wrong. Educators are all too aware, even on the basis of an honest self-knowledge, how children and young people are (or can be) unstable and fickle as they grow up. Don Bosco himself was in this respect a huge realist, almost a borderline pessimist, as a consequence of the Jansenist influence of his theological training that heavily emphasised the idea that the human person is a sinner and thus affected by wrong inclinations. Today it seems we find ourselves in the other extreme of a pure optimistic and romantic view (under the influence of Rousseau) on the 'natural [spontaneous] goodness' of the human person whereby we no longer dare to mention—although we do realise it—that on the moral level, the human person is surely vulnerable and does not automatically opt for the good, and at times takes a long path full of twists and turns and detours in deciding upon the good. The determination to prevent evil should therefore not degenerate into hard inflexibility with no attention for the vulnerability of children and young people that is made apparent in their personal biographies. Hence, Salesian reasonableness not only acknowledges the fragility of the educatee but also strives to get to know him or her better individually so that the educator can understand each one uniquely and let oneself be guided by that knowledge in the pedagogical treatment and 'measures', which must be handled with discretion and utmost respect. Reasonable treatment does not underestimate nor overload. Pedagogical reasonableness ensures that firmness never ends up in unmerciful hardness and roughness: it maintains 'moderation' and finds the right balance, or rather effects the right combination (compromise) between firmness and

21 Literally Don Bosco says: "Only in cases of immoral behaviour will the superiors be implacable. It is better to run the risk of expelling an innocent from the house than to retain someone who causes scandal." Cited by R. Biesmans, *De Magna Charta van het salesiaanse opvoedingssysteem. Hulpboekje*, 28.

gentleness. It lets itself be led by love that banishes fear as mentioned in the Bible, to which Don Bosco also explicitly refers: "There is no fear in love, but perfect love casts out fear; for fear has to do with punishment, and whoever fears has not reached perfection in love" (1 Jn 4:18).

This correct moderation likewise includes a pedagogically sound handling of punishments for violations and mistakes. That wisdom is based on different aspects: on the one hand, the mentioned factual fragility (finiteness) and ethical vulnerability of children and young people in their growth; on the other, the circumstances and forms of complicity of others within which the violation took place; and, last but not least, the seriousness of the violation. For when it involves serious violations, which are related to the prohibitions in the Decalogue we just outlined, an honest confrontation with the facts is desirable. However, a mere confrontation with the violation itself is insufficient. The guilty party must be given space to relate one's own story, not only about what has happened but also the context, the provocation and the reasons. One who commits an error should never be confined in one's guilt without being heard. A climate of attention and acknowledgement is needed, and all forms of threats and blackmail need to be avoided. With regard to sanctions, Don Bosco and the Salesian tradition are proponents of an education without punishment or, more nuanced, an education with as minimal punishment as possible. In '*Il sistema preventivo*' we read literally: "I say in all honesty: I dislike punishment. I do not find it pleasant to have to scold someone who fails with the threat of punishment: that is not my system!"[22] Corporal punishments are purely and simply out of the question, and today we can similarly say: even the so-called 'pedagogical trap' must be avoided. The fundamental principle of a reasonable education is that sanctions should be avoided as much as possible. Often and in spite of themselves, on the basis of their personal and contextual injuries, young people may be 'out of balance' but one should not lose sight of the emotionally humiliating impact of a punishment. Punishments that are given and implemented with the best intentions can cause a sense of hurt and humiliation amongst those who have to undergo them. And this can remain irreparably etched in their body and soul, causing all sorts of feelings of rancour and counter-revenge to arise. When educators are themselves marked by affective immaturity, they can take the violations by the educatee so personally—and it can also be a case of bullying by children or young people! —that they themselves are hurt and out of that hurt they react and punish.

22 Quoted by R. Biesmans, *Redelijkheid in de omgang met jongeren*, 96.

Whatever the (possibly understandable) basis of the hurt may be, it can never provide the correct motivation for a pedagogically reasonable interaction with the undesirable behaviour of a child or young person. Dealing with offences committed by children and young people in a reasonable manner requires self-control and deliberation (with oneself, but at times also with others). At the same time, such a reasonable treatment of those who fail or derail allays the fanaticism of the struggle against evil. Severe violations or forms of criminality amongst young people, for instance, unleash feelings of indignation and anger in the bystanders, even in the educators and assistants. Even though those feelings are understandable, and likewise suggest a correct awareness of integrity and values, one should still not be blind to the risk that those feelings may overturn into a heavy-handed battle against the inflicted evil, while neglecting the person—the often-injured young person—behind the mischief. Only when the educator elevates the emotion of his indignation, or even moral repulsion, to reason, is a humane, i.e., reasonable, sufficiently balanced and future-oriented treatment of the perpetrator possible.

In this regard, it is important to point out a way of sanctioning that is very powerful and at the same time very ambiguous. An educator can withhold one's *amorevolezza*, by stopping the expressions of benevolence and cordiality. Even in a Salesian context, one sometimes notices a plea to replace real, objective forms of punishment with this emotional deprivation: a firm look or a non-friendly gaze can bring about more than a slap or a threat of punishment, so it says. The insight into the force of heartfelt affection (*amorevolezza*), however, should make us implement this emotional punishment with utmost care. Approaching the educatee in an indifferent or negative manner can be more destructive than an objective punishment; it can be a form of emotional blackmail against which the child or the young person cannot defend itself. Hence, an objective but then reasonable or fair punishment is at times preferable to a hard emotional distancing, although the principle remains that punishment should be seldom. Not tackling children or young people for serious infringement on agreements and regulations likewise means not taking their freedom and responsibility seriously, but then the punishment must be in proportion to the degree of the offence or the inappropriate behaviour. Therefore, confrontation with and possible punishment for the offence must always contribute to recognising and developing a sense of responsibility, without crushing the educatee under this awareness. Gentleness and understanding, forms of *amorevolezza*, still remain. To put it differently, possible punishments must always be remedial, directed at reparation and growth. With Don Bosco, this strong conditional framing and relativising of punishment flows forth from his preference for a preventive approach, in contrast to the repressive approach. A preventive approach on the basis of monitoring and positive empowerment is today more than topical considering the unashamed plea from a clear segment in our society for 'law and order', namely for zero-tolerance and an unrelenting approach to young people (and adults) who go wrong and disturb the public order with their petty (and less petty) forms of unruliness, aggression and criminality. In the framework of Don Bosco's reason, and of those who follow him, a preventive approach underlies the importance they attach to confirmation and reward, which in turn can again be seen as expressions of *amorevolezza*. Admonition and censure for what has gone wrong can be a form of respect for the responsibility of the child or young person, with the necessary gentleness for their still underdeveloped self-determination. But that disapproval should never be absolutised into the only form of liability whereby the educatee gains a sense of total disapproval, with all its irreparable damage in the long term. Disapproval must remain limited in object, time and space, so that space remains for approval, praise and appreciation. Giving acknowledgement for the good that was done arouses in children and young people an unseen force of self-confidence and of commitment to the good as well.

Here, we would also like to refer to the Salesian tradition of the 'word in the ear' (*la parola all'orecchio*), namely the educator's personal whisper in the ear of the child or young person of a short word *en passant* (in passing) in the midst of a game or other activity. Its object can either be a disapproval or a confirmation and encouragement, a personal question or word of advice. The advantage is that it is private, and that is surely of huge importance as far as disapproval is concerned. Public reprimands risk humiliating the child or young person before the eyes of their companions and classmates, which can lead to depression or repressed anger. Hence the golden rule never to rebuke or reprimand an educatee in the company of one's peers, classmates, companions or friends. In this regard, Don Bosco used an expression from traditional ascetic (spiritual) literature: the 'fatherly' admonition should always take place *in camera caritatis* (literally 'in the room of love', meaning in confidence).

2.4. A 'Reasonable Enough Father'

We wish to expand these reflections on reasonableness as a method of education by dwelling for a moment on the reasonableness of the educator himself. We do so by arguing, in parallel with the 'good enough mother' in the field of *amorevolezza*, for the necessity of a 'reasonable enough father'.

Just as children and young people in their progressive, sometimes tortuous, path to emotional emancipation need a 'good mother'—a new 'family', in their growth towards self-determination on the basis of their own insights and visions, they need also a 'reasonable father' who does not take them in emotionally or manoeuvre them in a certain direction on the basis of his paternal authority or majority position but confronts them with the important matters of life from the objectivity of insightfully formulated and reasonably argued convictions. This brings us to the psychoanalytic idea of the 'paternal' agency, which breaks open the fusional world of participation and fusion—the world of unchastity (cf. supra)—so that the child, and the child in every human being, would break free from the mother (or 'maternal' agency) in order to turn outward to what is other than oneself, namely the world and especially others. The paternal agency makes it possible for the subject to free oneself from the submerged fusional, at the same time safe and captivating, participation. Note that paternal agency in principle does not refer to the actual father; although de facto it often refers to that actual father. The 'paternal' is represented by all kinds of institutions and people, including women and mothers, for example, single mothers and female educators. Specifically, it involves language, organised forms of life with their customs and the weight of their tradition, and other authoritative forms that incarnate certain understandings and modes of experience. They form the springboard for growing children and young people to gradually develop their own form of life, based on their own convictions and insights, in the wake of the pre-given ways of life, rules, institutions and models of behaviour. In ethics, also in Christian ethics, this is called the growth towards a 'formed conscience', or better an enlightened, formed and dialogical conscience and discernment (*AL* 303).

However, here again it is not a question of a 'totally reasonable father' but only of a 'reasonable enough father'. If the father figure (parent, educator), who interprets visions of values and points of view, is completely reasonable then the child or young person—according to their own developmental stage—is deprived of the possibility of arguing and discussing from the conviction of their own rightness which rests on a personal insight already gained. A parent, educator or supervisor who is completely wise, who determines the brilliance of truth and therefore knows with great certainty what is best, makes every educational conversation impossible. Subsequently, a growing person can never contribute anything because the educator is right beforehand. Then the educatee never again experiences the pleasure of knowing something him- or herself or of being right for once. To enter into a conversation (an exchange of ideas and words) with a totally reasonable, 'all-knowing' father is actually pointless. Only a finite father who is occasionally irrational or not entirely reasonable—not out of strategy but because, as a historically dependent being, he does not have all the wisdom—creates space for a true educational relationship. In this, not all insights come from one side, the educator, but also from the educatee, certainly from the young person, but also from the child, however limited and imperfect sometimes. The true conversation consists of listening and answering differently, according to the Jewish thinker Franz Rosenzweig (1886–1929),[23] and this is also the basis for every education, which not only makes people sensitive to values but also brings them to an understanding of values. From this flows a pedagogical authority with a human face, as opposed to an authoritarian, irrational and totalitarian authority marked by arbitrariness. It is an authority based on reasonableness, and at the same time it has a humble awareness of its finitude and limits. It wants to be reasonable, but it accepts that it does not have all the knowledge and wisdom and therefore is not an absolute guru. It is indeed a real, but at the same time humble and receptive authority that wants to learn from reality, and certainly from the children and young people who are on the way and in their growth need a reliable and reasonable, at the same time only sufficiently reasonable 'master'.

Last but not least, the fact that the educator sets himself up as a 'reasonable enough father' also means that he himself is not the first and last authority, but also subjects himself to reason, and consequently also to forms of authority that precede and exceed him. A 'reasonable educator' accepts that he is neither omnipotent nor omniscient, and thus that he may also be regulated and evaluated. Don Bosco himself also realised this. As the founder, and therefore

---

23 Cf. N.N. Glatzer, *Franz Rosenzweig: His Life and Thought*, (New York: Shocken Books, 1962).

the first and last 'authority', of the Oratory, he acknowledged the need to present his experiences and perceptions, even his difficulties and doubts, to his spiritual director, Don Cafasso, especially in periods of great stress or fatigue, and especially when he was accused of having mental health issues (just think of the episode when they wanted to put him in a psychiatric institution). It is significant that Don Cafasso explicitly advises Don Bosco to immerse himself in morality, not so much as a "rigid, inexorable code" but as a path to wisdom and balance in daily life, both in dealing with his boys and with his co-workers, especially the young Salesian fellow-brothers. Even though he wanted to go his own way with his educational work, he kept direct and regular contact with the bishop of Turin, as well as with the diocesan clergy, who sometimes made critical comments. He also accepted the input of his closest collaborators, in particular also of theologian Giovanni Borelli, a faithful *compagnon de route* (fellow traveller) during the first pastoral works and engagements. Besides, as a faithful Christian, Don Bosco constantly put himself under the authority of Scripture and of the Church (we cannot forget how the Pope obliged him to get involved in other matters than his boys). Despite going his own way from his charisma with an unmistakable stubbornness, he still did not shut himself up in his ivory tower, as if he had a direct line with God or the Holy Spirit, but he humbly accepted the mediations of ecclesiastical authority, Christian ethics, personal examination of conscience, spiritual guidance or supervision, which enabled him to question and test himself. This need for mediation of the educator's pedagogical authority is still valid today. No educator can be an educator alone, without other educators in the team, with the necessary exchanges and assessments, or through 'intervision', not only on the basis of one's own and mutually shared experiences but also under the authority of the Salesian pedagogical plan one uses, and of all kinds of new scientific insights (which, of course, one also approaches with critical caution), as well as of external forms of perpetual evaluation—however difficult they may be.

2.5. Integral Education as 'Aesthetics': Communities of Participation

Not everything has been said, however, about the aspect of reason and reasonableness in education, certainly not in the perspective of Don Bosco's view on integral education. So that reasonableness that originates in the (ethical and practical) 'laws' of reason could be effective, more still is needed than the law. We would like to call this the 'aesthetic dimension' of upbringing or education. We saw above how prohibitions form the indispensable conditions for love, even more how they only indicate the conditions for love without delineating and prescribing normatively how that love must acquire concrete shape.

For that positive delineation of love, children and young people do not so much need behavioural norms that prescribe how they must live and act humanely, which would tie up their 'freedom for', but rather they need suggestive examples, inspiring models, testimonies and qualitative experiences of others, that address and attract them without moralising them in a patronising way.[24] In that manner, they will strive to integrate the values that take shape in the examples and experiences in their own way, i.e., creatively, and substantiate them. They do not need normative models to copy or slavishly imitate when it comes to ethical growth toward human quality or meaningfulness, but rather 'cool' ways of experiencing things that can give them a taste for what makes life and living together worthwhile.[25] We can call this the aesthetic dimension of 'law and reason'—of ethics. It no longer concerns the bottommost boundary or the minimum of prohibitions, but rather the optimum or the quality of meaningful life and action, which in the Christian perspective is the fullness of love.

For the creative realisation of the meaningful quality of love, children and young people can and may call upon the contagious examples and behaviours lived out by their predecessors—parents and educators—in the context of 'living communities', in which the quality of love realistically takes shape.[26] It is by means of tradition, meaning to say by what has been handed down and consequently precedes us, that we can, with taste and conviction, make certain attitudes, modes of behaviour and lifestyles our own. Ethics and education

---

24 In the third part of this essay, see how, from a religious-Christian perspective, both the lives of the saints and the example of Jesus Christ himself have an important pedagogical role to play, especially in Don Bosco's vision of education.

25 M. Scheler, *Der Formalismus in der Ethik und die materiale Wertethik. Neuer Versuch der Grundlegung eines ethischen Personalismus*, (5th ed.), (Bern/München: Max Niemeyer, 1965), 560.

26 A. MacIntyre, *After Virtue. A Study in Moral Theory*, (London: Duckworth, 1981); S. Hauerwas, *Vision and Virtue. Essays in Christian Ethical Reflection*, (Notre Dame, US: University of Notre Dame Press, 1974).

can never be a one-man-show, a solipsistic affair. We are dependent on our predecessors in order to be able to grow towards moral sensitivity, truth and praxis. No one becomes ethically sensitive and proficient without parents and grandparents, family, relatives, educators and the wider community, out of which new people time and again receive the chance to discover and to tread into their path of life. It is precisely through this community life anchored in space and time that ethical aesthetics, which is indispensable in achieving a loved-filled living and acting, takes shape. In other words, it is not just important that people are able to participate in moral communities, it is as necessary as the air we breathe. In such moral communities, ethical quality is not underestimated. Ethical quality carries with it a stimulus by means of its beauty in order to grow towards that which is loving, each one according to his or her own possibilities and fragilities or limitations. Because of this participative character, we call these moral communities 'communities of participation'. In such communities of life, people throughout the generations share with each other's ethical inspiration and thus give a solid grounding to their own ethical commitment and make it bearable. Only by participating in concrete ethical projects, wherein the commitment of the whole person is involved—not only one's intellect, but also one's desire, feeling, fantasy, body and will—can children and young people acquire the chance to develop from the inside out a delicate taste for a love-filled life and its according actions. Whoever cannot share in values, modes of behaviour and life, and this in the double sense of co-experiencing and also co-constructing, can never acquire a sensitivity and taste for what is a meaningful and loving life. Without a community of participation, children and young people can never discover that virtue not only takes effort and sacrifices, but also the fact that it does one good. In that way, the link with *amorevolezza* becomes clear. On the ethical level, the community of participation is the expression of the original sheltering and encompassing affectivity and affection, and therefore of *amorevolezza*; stronger still, it is the condition of possibility and embedment of every education, in particular of ethical education.

For that purpose, every moral community must also be a 'narrative community', where one exchanges; where educator and educatee find each other and listen in a non-normative but suggestive, enriching, challenging way; where adults do not moralise from their experiential wisdom, but give witness and inspire, invite and literally 'pro-voke'. The narrative community issues a call to move forward, so that the 'pre-given' ethical heritage can take shape in a dynamic and even progressive way. An ethical narrative community is literally a community where people tell their story, and in so doing, they recuperate something as a community. It is also where the foundational stories with the experiential wisdom of the ancestors are not only narrated and discussed, but also celebrated in symbolic signs and rituals. As a narrative community, a community of participation always is and becomes an expressive community!

In this regard, we would like to point out the importance of eating together and of the family table, which are entirely in line with the Salesian family spirit. The starting point of my reflection is anecdotal. When, some time ago, I returned from Minster (Kent, UK) after a three-day training session, while waiting in line at the airport, I read an article in a newspaper on the decline of family meals and its impact on the social skills of children. A sociological study came to the conclusion that (especially in cities) 1 out of 10 adults no longer eat together with their children and that another 10 per cent eat together with their children only once a week. The increase of TV-meals on the sofa deprives children, according to another research, of vital skills. Children grow up and miss the opportunity to talk with adults, to exchange ideas, and to learn good manners. The decline of family meals is moreover linked with a health risk, namely an increased intake of high fat content food. This decline of family meals likewise runs parallel with a strong emphasis in schools and families and in popular culture (among others in teen magazines, weeklies, on TV and social media) on personal ambition (getting somewhere) and material success whereby the self-esteem of children is changing severely. We are getting generations of children and young people who risk being out of balance. Some have too low self-esteem (because they cannot reach the norms of ambition) and others have too high self-esteem precisely because they (are able to) go along with the ambition-ideology wherein attention is rather given to creating a circle of influence rather than striving for a circle of concern. In our neo-liberal societies, a person's value depends not only on his or her capacities or talents but also, and especially, on what he or she does with those capabilities and talents. This is literally 'meritocracy': thanks to effort and hard work, you earn influence, acquire success and are honoured.[27] The emphasis on material success and achieving something in life comes at the expense of establishing a sense of belonging and that leads to an inversion of fundamental values and its consequences. Our school and education systems, and our public culture

27 P. Verhaeghe, *Le délire néolibéral. Flexible, efficace et… dérangé*, (Bruxelles: ASP (Academic and Scientific Publishers), 2013).

and mentality turn values on their heads whereby essential values are affected. Children are told that they 'will belong somewhere' when they achieve material success, while they first have to belong somewhere—emotionally and spiritually—in order to draw out confidence and to actualise their personal development and ambition. Apparently, we are gradually paying a hefty price for dissolving the connectedness that serves as the first and essential source of value-development. As a society, in this way we risk losing the beneficial effects of sharing a meal around the table. Eating together has, since the earliest times, been the most formative way of building a sense of togetherness and facilitating conversation across the generations.

This challenges us to focus on eating together, working together and relaxing together, in the Salesian spirit, as the context for the development of values and norms—of reason and law—and certainly not to allow that the 'family spirit' be displaced from its central position by the growing neoliberal emphasis on competency development. And neither can we ignore the importance that the Salesian tradition attaches to feasts. Here, one loves to cite the mischievous statement that is ascribed to Don Bosco himself to reinforce its authority and importance: "If there are no feasts, you have to create them." They make it possible for one to participate via emotion and imagination—detached from external moralising obligations—in the implied values, and to gradually become aware of them and appreciate them. Feasts also create family spirit and belonging, not only or primarily as a means to education but especially as a goal and expressive value in and of itself.

A Mountain Hike (midrash of a Don Bosco dream)

To conclude this second part, we paraphrase a dream of Don Bosco, to evoke what is meant by an ethics of growth for young (and less young) people on their way. Both the perspective of the desirable or the meaningful, as well as what is most possible and attainable are kept in mutual tension. Reason plays an important role in this tension through the boundary rules of the second tablet of the ten commandments.

Ethics and education, as guidance, can be described as a mountain hike: not remaining indecisively non-committal or merely fretting and fuming, but to go on a hike, not just wherever but with a prospect before you, a goal that is well worth it. Going along life's way is not an aimless wandering about but having a horizon—literally a 'panoramic view'—before you that not only reaches farther but also higher and invites you to go to the top. A dynamic life is constantly aiming for the top. Sometimes it is fairly visible, sometimes not, but the top is always there. There is always the prospect and the appeal to the meaningful as the goal (*Zielgebot*).

To successfully accomplish a mountain hike, one needs a guide or a map. These are the fundamental values and norms that indicate direction like a compass. Just think of non-violence ('you shall not kill'), mutual equality ('you shall not steal'), trust and tenderness ('you shall not commit adultery'), authenticity ('you shall not bear false witness'). But you also need equipment and an outfit: thick-soled boots, two pairs of woollen socks, a backpack with provisions, eye protection against the cold, sunglasses against bright light, a walking pole, and so on.

Upon departure, it turns out that a number of young people do not see the top. For them, it is hidden in the mist. Others think that the top, or the meaningful of purpose, is somewhere else and therefore have a different view regarding the way to the top. Moreover, there are young people who have good intentions, but have no boots or have only one pair of socks or not enough substantial provisions. These are young people who, because of circumstances, are not always well-equipped in life. However, even they are called to go on the mountain hike and become full human beings.

But some among them will never be able to reach the top. Should they then remain below or be left behind, in the assumption that they are indeed not capable? Should we then abandon them and tell them they do not count? Does it suffice that we provide them with only a kind of occupational therapy at the foot of the mountain so that they will not be any source of harm to themselves or to the community? Or should we indeed invite them to begin the hike and urge them to grow in the direction of the top by making sure that they have two pairs of socks or by giving them a map? Even though that will not always be helpful because they perhaps cannot read well. Shouldn't we then be near them in any case, to literally assist them, so that during their mountain hike they can reach what they are capable of reaching, or even something more?

Some will perhaps succeed in climbing almost to the top. Perhaps, they have already reached a panorama of a certain quality. For a number of young people that is very good, more than good even, although they do not reach the goal of the meaningful. Others only come halfway, which is already something. This is not the 'truly good' or the *vere bonum*, but a 'lesser good', a *minus bonum*. And note well that this limited good is not simply a shortcoming and lack, but a real good which for them in their situation of incompleteness and incapacity, is the achievable and therefore the best possible and attainable. Or if young people only succeed in reaching a quarter of the way, they surely did not reach the *vere bonum* (the truly good) or the goal of the meaningful but indeed a smaller *minus bonum*, a smaller, lesser good, but nevertheless a good. In that, these young people are already saved and redeemed. Precisely for that reason, we should not abandon these young people at the foot of the mountain, or at the first stopover. They are indeed able to do more. They need a little push in the direction of the top, in order to climb up higher.

A realistic growth ethics, according to the 'law of gradualness'[28] and with an eye to the meaningful, employs mercy in order to not demand the meaningful so unrelentingly in all circumstances that some drop out because they cannot do it and just sit at the side of the mountain path or not even begin the hike. That is dramatic. It is precisely in the name of the Gospel that brings redemption and healing that we, on an ethical level, also have to save and heal young people. A growth ethics leaves in all discretion its own lofty standpoint and thinks and feels from the standpoint of the other, in this case that of young people, and their real and, to be sure, sometimes limited possibilities. That is why we plead, in the name of Jesus Christ whom we confess as our Saviour, in the footsteps of Don Bosco, for an ethics of the attainable, in the framework of an ethics of the meaningful, that means the fullness of love.

28 Cf. *FC* and *AL*.

3. *'Religione'*

Ensouled and Inspiring Education

The third pillar in the Salesian education project is 'religion' (*religione*). With this, we reach the dimension of meaning and spirituality in addition to the dimensions of emotionality and rationality.

There is no doubt that with Don Bosco his Christian faith lies at the foundation for his choice for young people, with particular attention to the vulnerable ones amongst them. His Christian faith as the anchoring of his educational interests was self-explanatory for him, but this should not be equated with thoughtlessness. After all, he had to struggle with the secularists in the Italy of the second half of the 19th century, who attempted to force their points of view in social and political life. In our secular, post-confessional society, it is no longer self-evident to raise religion as the foundation and inspiration for education. However, the present-day post-secular religious and ideological pluralism, namely the confrontation with new forms of spirituality and movements of revival, again puts the ensuing question of religion on the map. In the same way, the present renewed post-confessional attention to meaning and spirituality invites us to not shy away from Christian meaning as the soul and inspiration for the Salesian education project. On the contrary, we need to provide it again with all chances for success. Throughout our search, it will be clear how the Christian faith is both the anthropological and theological foundation, as well as the signpost, for an education in the spirit of Don Bosco.

One more important remark before we start our analysis and reflection on *religione*. On the one hand, *religione* is the foundation and inspiration, or soul and motivation, of the Salesian educational project. On the other hand, it is also an integrative perspective and goal of Don Bosco's pedagogical concept as a project of Christian education. Don Bosco's expression about the purpose of education is well known, namely, to raise his boys (children, young people) to be honest and responsible citizens and good Christians (*onesto cittadino e buon cristiano*). This means that when our discourse focuses on the inspiration for the educator, it applies *mutatis mutandis* (once the necessary changes are made) to the educatee and to the intent of education. Now and then, this will be recalled. But even if it is not explicitly stated, it remains valid that the soul of education refers also to the educational 'objective' for children and young people in the educational process.

3.1. Integral Concept of Human Person with Space for Spiritual Meaning and Religion

Before we describe and analyse the particular religious inspiration and perspective of the Salesian pedagogical project, we first would like to emphasise the essential character of the spiritual and religious dimension of meaning in a general sense. An integral or holistic view of humanity avoids all reduction of being humane to a mere autonomous dynamism whereby the human person is the only active creator of meaning. The Salesian pedagogical project is entirely in line with integral personalism (Louis Janssens),[1] as promoted by the Second Vatican Council (*Gaudium et Spes*, 1965, nos. 12–22, 51). This integral personalism recognises all the dimensions of the human person in their interrelatedness: one's uniqueness and historicity; one's relationship with oneself, nature and the world, the other and society, and what transcends one's existence. The Salesian pedagogical project transcends a narrow individualistic and anthropocentric image of the human and pays homage candidly to human openness for the transcendence or literally the 'meta-physical', i.e., 'beyond-the-physical'. And this openness involves the surpassing of oneself towards the other, whereby this other involves not only

1 L. Janssens, 'Personalist Morals', in: *Louvain Studies*, 3 (1970–71) 1, 5–16; ID., 'Artificial Insemination: Ethical Considerations', in: *Louvain Studies*, 8 (1980–81), 1, 3–29; R. Burggraeve, 'The Holistic Personalism of Professor Magister Louis Janssens', in: *Louvain Studies*, 27(2002)1, 29–38.

a relative but also a radical otherness. We describe this dynamism as the metaphysical openness of the human person, in the sense that in its 'soul', the human is marked by the ability to transcend the physical, the empirical, the mere inner-worldly. The meaning that is thus intended involves the ultimate significance of existence in this world, even though that meaning surpasses the world. Moreover, this encompassing meaning displays a future-oriented character whereby ultimate meaning acquires a utopian dimension. With Schillebeeckx, we can label this as a concept of totality that conveys a global horizon of meaning.[2] Among others, it makes the human capable of finding a bearable way of dealing with experiences of fiasco and failure, suffering and death, so that these do not have the final word (more on this later, where it will turn out that this describes but one dimension of religion). Consequently, life becomes promising, and people can experience it as meaningful, good, liberating and consoling.

Denying this openness for transcendence and encompassing meaning of human existence does injustice to the essential dimension of our humanity. This applies as well to education, which damages itself by approaching the educatee only as an immanently earthly creature that in its relationship to itself and to the other is the first and last creator of meaning, the alpha and omega of sense and nonsense. The pedagogical project in the spirit of Don Bosco radically rejects such a closed image of the human. In contrast, it honours an integral or holistic image of the human whereby the existentially spiritual openness to transcendent meaning is not shied away from but actually takes central stage as an integrating perspective of 'meaning-fullness'. For Don Bosco, its further elaboration was self-evidently Christian. Not only because he was born and raised in the Christian faith but also because it belonged to the cultural context of Italian society in the 19th century even though clear secularist counter-voices already arose.

Today we live more and more in a secularised or secularising and post-confessional situation as well as in a context of increasing ideological pluralism, not only with more religions but also with non-religious forms of spirituality. The perspective of totality on meaning expresses itself in and through a huge diversity of religions and non-religious views on life, worldviews and general

---

2 E. Schillebeeckx, *The Collected Works of Edward Schillebeeckx. Volume VI. Jesus: An Experiment in Christology*, (London: Bloomsbury Publishing, 2014), 609–610.

life theories. Humans attempt therein to express what ultimately inspires existence and what makes life worth living, literally 'meaning-full'. Even so-called, radically secular freethinking humanism is such a particular system of meaning and is not to be qualified negatively as non-religious or atheist. We also are cognisant today of forms of esoteric spirituality that provides people with perspectives and methods to discover their lives as meaningful or to make them so. All these modes of meaning, even the non-religious systems of meaning, reveal themselves more and more as a very particular form of faith. They are about convictions which, upon closer inspection, can never entirely be tested scientifically or rationally, although certain parts of the life views demonstrate a certain plausibility. No one thrives without a form of faith! It is the ground of hope without which a humane and liveable human life becomes impossible and people end up in neurotic conditions or seek refuge in all sorts of *mirabilia*, horoscopes, meditation techniques and mindfulness, or all kinds of so-called spiritual lifestyles with their alternative vegetarian diets, body practices and holistic health models.

Hence the need today for interreligious and inter-ideological (inter-worldview or inter-convictional) dialogue, even in upbringing and education. This dialogue needs to take a double movement: *ad intra*, i.e., a loyal and critical conversation with one's own, *in casu* Christian tradition and *ad extra*, i.e., a candid but equally critical conversation with other worldviews and convictions, both religious and non-religious, even post- and anti-religious. Every religion is particular, and it is precisely out of this particularity that a religion accedes another ideology (system of meaning and convictions) or religion and enters in conversation with it honestly and courageously. It does not, however, allow one's own individuality to evaporate in a neutral universality and likewise does not have the pretence to raise one's own uniqueness as the only universal truth to which the other particularities are then reduced. According to the Jewish philosopher Emmanuel Levinas,[3] this conversation with the other needs to be a conversation without compromises and cheap concessions. It is a conversation that does not rest on strategy or cunning, tact or diplomacy, nor on formal tolerance or even on sympathy and friendship. It concerns a dialogue that does not sacrifice one's own ideology of meaning and convictions to the fascinating exoticism of the other, but that, starting from the conversation with one's own tradition, is based on attention

3 E. Levinas, *Alterity and Transcendence,* Tr. M.B. Smith, (New York: Columbia University Press, 1999).

and watchfulness to who the other truly is. In this way, we can also better understand and deepen our own ideology. It likewise means acknowledging and naming that which is irreconcilable and irresolvable and preventing it resulting in forms of violence, denial, domination. It concerns "the search for a proximity beyond the ideas exchanged, a proximity that lasts even after dialogue has become impossible."[4] A true learning process that must transpire both courageously as well as non-violently.[5] This means that in Don Bosco's sprit, education takes seriously the dimension of meaning, spirituality and religion as an 'anthropological constant' (Schillebeeckx).[6] We can never neglect the source from which Salesian education derives its inspiration and perspective, as is summarised in the life motto of Don Bosco: *Da mihi animas*. What ultimately concerns him is not only the material, affective, intellectual, professional and social well-being of his young people, but also and especially their spiritual development. For him, an authentic religious life does not stand separated from all the rest. It actually forms the embedment and inspiration for the other dimensions of human well-being. One indeed also strives for and develops those other dimensions in the name of the Christian view on integral meaning and comprehensive and ultimate wholeness. Hence, spiritual and religious upbringing belong to the constitutive goals of the Salesian pedagogical project. Cutting away education from the spiritual, meaning and religious dimension of human existence, as can be found today in various modern and postmodern pedagogical views, does fundamental injustice to the concept of integral education that is so dear to Don Bosco and the Salesian tradition. Moreover, annulling the particular Christian interpretation of meaning, transcendence and religion in Don Bosco by reducing it to a general and neutral form of spirituality does equal injustice to the Salesian education project. On the other hand, this emphasis on the Christian particularity of '*religione*' in Don Bosco does not mean that there would be no place in the

4 Ibid., 87.

5 For further reflection on interreligious and inter-convictional or interideological dialogue, see our publication: 'Dialogue of Transcendence: A Levinasian Perspective on the Anthropological-Ethical Conditions for Interreligious Dialogue', in: *Journal of Communication & Religion*, 37 (2014), n. 1, spring, 2–28.

6 The anthropological constant refers to the essential dimensions of the human person adequately and integrally understood, as we also find in the already mentioned integral personalism (Louis Janssens). Cf. D. Minch, 'Re-examining Edward Schillebeeckx's Anthropological Constants: An Ontological Perspective', in: S. Van Erp, C. Alpers, C. Cimorelli (eds.), *Edward Schillebeeckx and the Theology of Public Life*, (London: Bloomsbury T&T Clark, 2016), 27–30.

Salesian pedagogical project for conversation with other particular systems of meaning (worldviews) and religions. Such place is present precisely on the basis of the Salesian thought on assistance, namely openness for and nearness to the young people the way they are and the way they come to us.

3.2. From the Human Desire as a Child of Indigence and Abundance

In the search of an interpretive key of religion that can do justice to both Don Bosco's concern, seeking inspiration and perspective for integral education, as well as to current challenges, thanks to Emmanuel Levinas we find inspiration in Plato's interpretation of human desire (*eros).*[7]

Plato describes *eros* as a "child of indigence and abundance".[8] This suggests that *eros* as desire is driven by a double movement, namely need and lack on the one hand, and fullness and abundance on the other. At first sight, our human striving from the experience of shortage and lack, namely from the negativity of what we do not have and yet need (appetite). Hence, we do not remain affixed in *ataraxia* rigidly coinciding with ourselves, but in a dynamic way—avid and passionate, driven—go in search for that which can resolve and fulfil our shortage. Plato, however, also discovers in human *eros* another movement, namely a fullness that strives to 'pour out' itself. Desire does not lock itself up but moves outwards, not because it is in need of something else, but in order to give itself to the other. Levinas describes this as a qualitative dynamic of infinity, distinct from the quantitative idea of eternity, namely as something that lasts and endures (for ever and ever and ever...). He characterises the qualitative infinity dynamics as the "insatiable desire—not because it corresponds to an infinite hunger, but because it is not an appeal for food. This desire is insatiable, but not because of our finitude."[9] This desire beyond need:

---

7 The Jewish philosopher Emmanuel Levinas (1905–1995) repeatedly (cf. infra) refers to Plato's view of *eros* to understand the multiple, paradoxical dynamics of human desire.

8 E. Levinas, *Proper Names (Essays)*, Tr. M.B. Smith, (Stanford (CA): Stanford University Press, 1996), 113.

9 E. Levinas, *Totality and Infinity. An essay on exteriority*, Tr. A. Lingis, (The Hague/Boston/London:Martinus Nijhoff Publishers, 1979), 63.

> Is a more within a less that awakens with its most ardent and most ancient flame a thought given to thinking more than it thinks. Here is a desire of a different order than that of affectivity or the hedonic activity by which the desirable is invested, attained, and identified as an object of need. ...The negativity of the 'in-' of infinity hollows out a desire that could not be filled, that nourishes itself from its own growth, that exalts itself as desire, and that grows distant from satisfaction insofar as it approaches the desirable. A desire that does not identify as need does. A desire without hunger, and also without end [*sans faim et aussi sans fin*]; a desire for the infinite as desire for what is beyond being, which is stated in the word 'dis-inter-estedness'. This is transcendence and desire for the Good.[10]

The paradox, however, according to Plato, is that in both forms of *eros*, poverty and wealth go together. Not only is it actually about two forms of desire, but both are also marked by poverty and wealth, meaning to say by an interaction between both, albeit in different ways. In its reaching towards the other, desire is also a way of enjoying, namely a way to acquire independence via dependence. In the relationship to the object that must offer solace, desire also finds satisfaction. Desire fulfils itself as the wealth of poverty. We enjoy what we eat, we savour what we need in order to live and live well. I am happy with my needs; I live of my needs and my needs themselves provide me with pleasures and gratifications as well. Without hunger, you cannot enjoy delicious food. Perhaps we deplore our neediness, but this sadness is not final because it is transformed into the pleasure of devouring the other in and through that devouring itself. In other words, finitude is at first sight perhaps negative, but upon closer inspection again not. We are not merely 'thrown', as Heidegger suggests; our finitude is not without delight. The striving that ensues from finitude does not only express emptiness but also the fullness of the striving itself.

On the other hand, as child of wealth, *eros* is also marked by need and thus by the coincidence of wealth and poverty but now as the indigence of wealth: "Need is the poverty as source of riches, in contrast with desire, which is the poverty of riches."[11] The wealth of desire that is insatiable manifests itself as the need—the inner impulse—to develop oneself and to give to the other to

---

10 E. Levinas, *God, death, and time*, Tr. B.G. Bergo, (Stanford (CA), Stanford University Press, 2000), 221.

11 Levinas, *Totality and Infinity*, 115.

which it reaches: as insatiable longing it strives not for gratification of itself, since it is a desire without deficiency. Well then, precisely as desire that is not directed at gratification of itself, it can direct itself entirely to the other than itself for the sake of that other. "The desire without satisfaction hence takes cognisance of the alterity of the other."[12] This is also a form of hunger, albeit a special form. The desirable, namely the other, does not satisfy my desire, it hollows me, nourishing me somehow with new hungers, namely the hunger to be for and with the other. Here, desire turns out to be disinterestedness, goodness, radical generosity, "insatiable compassion", as Marmeladova in Dostoevsky's 'Crime and Punishment' looks at Raskolnikov, the murderer, in his despair.[13] This desire as a need, which needs to go beyond every need, burning with a fire that is not rooted in need and that is not extinguished by saturation.[14] "The relation with the other challenges me, empties me of myself and keeps on emptying me by showing me ever new sources. I did not know I was so rich, but I don't have the right to keep anything anymore."[15] Because of this surplus, Levinas calls this goodness full of desire a hunger that never ceases, rather a hunger that infinitely increases: "the marvel of infinity in the finitude".[16] This means that insatiable desire is a fullness that is at the same time need and necessity, namely a fullness that is not fullness enough, a nearness to the other that is never near enough. This infinite desire—a desire that 'infinitises' itself—reveals an inverted world: the emptiness of fullness, a fullness that bursts open, a fullness that does not take delight in itself and thus does not suffocate but turns itself 'extra-versively' towards the other than itself, without stalling. And this not because it needs the other but because in all its wealth it attunes itself—rather because in all its wealth, in spite of itself, it is attuned—to the other with the intention of acknowledging, confirming and promoting the other. Hence, this desire never rests in itself but it deepens itself time and again: every end is a new beginning!

---

12 E. Levinas, 'Philosophy and the Idea of Infinity', in A. Lingis (ed.), *Collected Philosophical Papers*, (Dordrecht/Boston/Lancaster: Martinus Nijhoff Publishers, 1987), 47–59, 56.

13 E. Levinas, *Humanism of the Other*, Tr. N. Poller, (Urbana & Chicago, University of Illinois Press, 2003), 27, 30.

14 Ibid., 33.

15 Ibid., 30.

16 Ibid., 34.

3.3. Religion Gives Expression to Finitude and Infinity

This analysis of the double dimension of *eros* as desire, with its paradoxical relationship between poverty and wealth, can simply be applied to religion as a human phenomenon. With this we go against the still too often used theory, namely that religion would be above all a doctrine or system of truths. This argument is criticised and rightly so. The positive reverse side of this critique is that religion primarily has an existential significance in the sense that it is anchored anthropologically in the desire of humans, in their viscerality, in their physical emotionality. Then only afterwards can it develop into a system of doctrines or a worldview. And according to the bidimensionality of human desire, as we have outlined above, we can state that religion as experiential reality is also bidimensional. On the one hand, religion is the answer to our finitude, or rather a way of dealing with this finitude by making use of all sorts of stories, symbols and rituals. Religion thus as a "need for salvation".[17] The paradox is that this need-religion, just as this applies to all human need, is equally a source of gratification. Even though we are dependent on salvation, in and through our striving for and our experience of salvation (by God, Christ… as Saviour), we also reach independence and fullness—call it 'heaven' if you will—not only as a reward but in and through the experience of salvation itself, already now in this world as a 'valley of tears'. This will be made even clearer in the next part of our argument. Experiencing religion also as need likewise brings forth joy: the wealth of poverty.

On the other hand, religion also gives expression to our infinity that we have discovered in the 'infinitising' of desire. For Plato and Levinas (and for Augustine and many others) it is so that *eros* as the 'sublime desire', i.e., as desire for and dedication to the other than oneself, puts us precisely on track to the Infinite, *in concreto* to the transcendent Other One. The interhuman desire of the one for the other is, for Don Bosco, literally '*à-Dieu*'— 'unto God'. The idea of the Infinite, as in the Infinite in me, is God dividing up the consciousness beyond myself, towards and for the other. The idea of the Infinite, literally the non-finite within the finite, is the idea of the Good in me: "A passivity, or passion, in which desire is recognised, in which the 'more in the less' awakens with its most ardent, most noble, and most ancient flame."[18] Below, we shall encounter concretely this religion, this self-surpassing desire,

17 Levinas, *Humanism of the Other*, 29.
18 Levinas, *Of God Who Comes to Mind*, 67.

in Don Bosco's Christian faith in divine love, the *agapē*, which has been poured out into our soul by the Holy Spirit and inspires us. This reveals how the person is a soulmate of God, without thereby losing sight of the fact that the human being substantiates this ensoulment as a finite and sinful being—which accurately sheds light on the need of the human person for salvation and healing. Likewise, we should not lose sight of the fact that this proximity, or rather this intimacy and immanence of God as the Spirit-of-Love-in-us, also remains transcendent, wholly other and inaccessible. In other words, God keeps on withdrawing into One's invisible, infinite mystery.

Before we further go into the double dimension of religion, just as Don Bosco has made it the inspiration and perspective of his life and of his pedagogical work, we pose one more consideration. However clearly distinct the two forms of religion may be, based on human finitude and infinity, in the specific forms of religion—in our case, of Christianity—they cannot be separated. All expressions and shapes of religion, i.e., all narratives, forms of prayer, symbols and rituals, including the truths of faith or the so-called 'dogmas', are marked by both dimensions. They give shape to both the dimension of finitude as well as of infinity in religion, even though the one form expresses more and the other less of both dimensions, depending on the circumstances and the context wherein the religious form is experienced. In all forms of meaning, spirituality and religion, however particular they may be, there remain aspects of emptiness and fullness, and of their mutual connection: the wealth of poverty and the poverty of wealth. Hence in our further exploration and discussion of the Salesian pedagogical project, particularly in the last section of this third part on '*religione*', we cannot—and shall not—separate the religious forms but treat them as integrated, paying attention to how both relate to the finitude as well as to the infinity of human desire.

3.4. Religious Meaning from the Perspective of Human Finitude

Since the human is a needy being, not only materially, relationally and socially but also on a fundamental level, the different forms of spirituality, religiosity and 'confessionality' present themselves as attempts to provide for the existential and spiritual neediness of the human person. Religions explicitly want to give an answer to human finitude that shows itself especially in all forms of powerlessness and suffering, including mortality and death, which seem to question all endeavours for happiness and meaning.

Religion has always been an answer to human needs, however great or small. People travel to pilgrimage places to pray to Mary to intercede for them, to spare them from danger and sickness, or to heal them, not only bodily but also in their relations and, last, but not least, spiritually. They go and pray for themselves and for others, in the awareness that there is much that they need and that they do not have the power to provide for it themselves. They are aware that they are in need of help and salvation; they feel 'salvation-needy'. Hence, they—humbly—step out of themselves and turn towards the 'other'—so-called 'supernatural'— world to find solace there for that which lies beyond their own power.

Unfortunately, some believers and often unbelievers or especially post-believers have looked rather contemptuously at this 'need-religion' as if it were an inferior form of religion. They actually find that in such a need-religion, God is reduced to a problem-solver, a magical power, or a means and an instrument of one's own self-development. This critical approach through 'religiously correct' thinking certainly has its merits, as will be made apparent below, but it can also be an expression of haughty arrogance. From their exalted ivory towers, they think they know better, until they are naturally affected by one or the other disease or major accident whereby they end up in misery and defeat. And then they often find it no longer beneath them to light candles before the image of Our Blessed Lady on the mantel or in a chapel.
An honest and, at the same time, humble interpretation of religion, however, is not ashamed of acknowledging this need-religion even though it is not given the final word (as will become apparent here below). This also applies to the Christian faith that is not ashamed of speaking about healing and salvation from God-in-Christ, with Mary and the saints as mediators and advocates. In his earthly life, Jesus was indeed involved with the finitude, fragility and wounds of ordinary people. Hence, he healed the sick and freed people from all sorts of awkward situations like possession by 'evil spirits' (cf. infra). It is no coincidence that Christ is called the Saviour in imitation of God who in the Old Testament is called '*goël*', 'the one who disentangles'.

For Don Bosco the Christian religion, just as he had received it in his youth and had deepened it during his theological training, was strongly characterised by what we today would call a form of supernaturalism. There, Jesus Christ as Saviour took centre stage as well as the position of eternal life to which people in this life were headed. The idea of eschatology or the ultimate goal of life is placed above or beyond this world in the 'super-natural'. The fullness of life is not of this world because of the finitude of this world and of the human existence. Hence, the emphasis on 'the last things' or heaven as redemption and fulfilment, and on the huge importance of our preparation in this earthly valley of tears as a way of not only anticipating but also deserving the life in God. Moreover, this gift of and the way towards supernatural life is mediated by the Church and the sacraments, mainly the Eucharist. Don Bosco assigns a special role to the divine providence and to the mediation of Mother Mary, Help of Christians to be a refuge for children and young people in all need. In this maternal protection, which is characteristic of the Catholic tradition, incarnates also what he means by the tangible and sensitive love of *amorevolezza*.

However positive this religiosity may be, we should not be blind to the risk of a certain one-sidedness, whereby the category of salvation is interpreted in a strongly individualistic manner. In the history of theology this tendency acquired the name of soteriologism, which places a one-sided emphasis on redemption of the individual. The human being stands alone before God.[19] In order to be able to speak of Jesus as salvation, all emphasis must first be put on the radical situation of the calamity of the human person: *homo absconditus, contingens et lapsus* (man hidden, dependent and fallen). The existential calamity, as experienced through finitude (and moral weakness and imperfection),[20] does not only involve humanity in general, but also and especially every human being individually. However realistic and honest it may be, this soteriologism leads inadvertently to individualism. Every person is as an individual inadequate, powerless, immersed in existential (and moral) fragility. At the same time, the relationship between God and humans is reduced to an opposition between human fragility and finitude, and God's divine power and mercy. The religious life comes to be expressed in the 'I' form: 'I' am the one in darkness and misery. The only thing left for the person is to turn oneself in trusting faith to God and to surrender oneself unconditionally

19 Cf. Anslem, 'Coram Deo', in *Cur Deus homo? (Why Did God Become Man?)*.

20 Here we consider sin rather as personal imperfection and fragility. We'll focus on the ethical and relational meaning of sinfulness in the connection between 'infinity' and (Christian) 'religion'.

to God's saving grace that by the power of that grace can heal my emptiness and failures. If this is the only way to experience the relationship with God and Christ (and Mary), then it inevitably leads to a fideistic experience of faith. As a little soul, I can only entrust myself in an unconditional and humble act of total surrender to God my Master and Saviour.

We cannot be blind to the outcome of infantilising of the faithful as human beings. The importance of personal responsibility for oneself disappears all too much, if at all, into the background. The person is reduced to an immature child that, in its situation of need out of which it cannot remove itself, can only look up in utter dependence and can open itself up without reserve, but also without any merit, to the grace that only God can give. Here, not only is the immaturity of the person emphasised but at the same time a very specific image of God's omnipotence and transcendence is put forth. God's power to face and meet the human need for salvation is inclined to become the measure of God's greatness and majesty. God's transcendence becomes confined in the role of parent—at times strict, at times lenient—towards the person as child. In this manner, injustice is done both towards God as well as towards humans. In a one-sided or exclusively practised 'need-and-salvation-religion', there is little room for God's glory in His creation, no less for the glory of humans as creatures. Where is the strength and the power of humans as the image and likeness of God (see Gen 1:26; Psalm 8), as God's co-creator and representative on earth, who can be approached for their responsibility and talents (see Matt 25)? Where is the special privilege of humans to live in a partnership of trust and covenant with God? Only when 'need-religion' is coupled with a 'responsibility-religion' do humans stand eye to eye with God, become partners of God who have an indispensable role to play in the covenant, now no longer only out of their bottomless emptiness but also out of their powerful fullness and divine infinity with which they are marked in their souls (cf. infra). We can label this as the need for a religion for adults. For free and responsible beings who stand upright before God and from that independence come to face Him (and the others and the world, as will become clear). That is one of the essential goals, not only of religious education but of all education!

It is remarkable that Don Bosco did not fall into the trap of infantilising soteriologism. By emphasising the path and pursuit of holiness, and thus the personal responsibility of young people, he unwittingly linked the idea of (divine) redemption with an emancipatory dynamic, without having to lead to a moralising form of religion (by ways of penetrating and manipulating the personal moral conscience). This ties in with the idea of the 'wealth of poverty', which applies not only to *eros* but also to religion. Religion as redemption does not allow the fragile and vulnerable human being to sink into one's lostness, but precisely through redemption it awakens the fragile human being to resilience and independence. Pedagogically, religion becomes a source of confidence and hope: no one is lost forever. However fragile and hurt, there is healing and growth and future for every child, every young person! In the Salesian pedagogical plan, therefore, the Christian religion of salvation is the theological source and inspiration for an educational 'ethics of growth'.[21]

3.5. Religious Meaning from the Perspective of Human Infinity

The perspective of an educational growth ethic indicates that, for Don Bosco, the Christian faith is not only 'child of poverty' and expresses human finitude, but also 'child of wealth' and equally expresses human infinity. We want to pay full attention to this now from the way we also find it with Don Bosco regularly, especially in '*Il sistema preventivo*' and his 'Letter from Rome, 1884'. Above all it became clear how the fullness of noble *eros* has everything to do with longing for the other for the sake of the other. On the basis of his Christian faith, Don Bosco invariably expresses this altrocentric love with the word '*caritas*', which denotes both charity and the unconditional love of God: '*agapē*'.

To be sure, religion is always a search for an answer to human deficiency and finitude, which likewise takes shape in the symbolic order of signs and rituals in the case of the sacraments, as was made clear above. But religion, in particular the Christian religion, is not to be reduced to that. Not only God is the Infinite, but even the human person is marked by and is bearer of infinity. To be authentic, Christian religion should give and wants to give expression to that reality. As creature and image of God, the human person is not only marked by all sorts of forms of fragility and brokenness; humans are just as much ensouled by the Infinite. Thanks to this divine plan, the human person is

---

21 R. Burggraeve, *An Ethics of Mercy. On the Way to Meaningful Living and Loving*, (Peeters: Leuven-Paris-Bristol (CT), 2016), 17–139, especially 105–139 (Chapter IV: A 'Pro-vocative' Ethics of Growth and Gradualness).

in this world a representative and sacrament of God. This means that religion does not only have to do with human weakness but also and especially with human strength: in the finite person resides the Infinite in such a way that the Infinite moves the finite beyond itself towards another, the other, for the sake of the other.

3.5.1. Pedagogical 'caritas' (love of neighbour)

What is immediately striking when we scrutinise the way in which Don Bosco motivates his commitment to the young from his Christian faith is that he does not put forward any great or spectacular theological reflections, but very simply refers to charity or '*carità*' as he invariably calls it in Italian. His commitment to youth, especially poor and vulnerable children and young people, is for him without question a form of 'pedagogical charity', or better 'pedagogical love of neighbour' (to avoid a purely 'charitable' interpretation). He himself testifies to this in his 'Letter from Rome':

> What I am writing here are the words of one who loves you intimately in Jesus Christ. ...You know how much I love my boys. You know what I have suffered and endured for them in the course of a good forty years, and how much I endure and suffer even now. How much hardship, how much humiliation, how much opposition, what all persecution to give them bread, shelter, teachers and above all to provide for the salvation of their souls. For those who make up the affection of all my life I have done all I could and can.[22]

In the expressive glow of this commitment and dedication,[23] the *amorevolezza* without a doubt also resounds, revealing at the same time the direct link between charity (love of neighbour) and pedagogical love. And let us not forget that all that we will say further about the anchoring of this pedagogical love in the *caritas*—'charity' for Don Bosco also represents a pedagogical tool and, above all, is objective and a goal of education as a learning process to become a 'fair and honest citizen and good Christian'.

---

22 R. Biesmans, *De Magna Charta van het salesiaanse opvoedingssysteem. Hulpboekje*, 3, 13–14.

23 In order to avoid the danger of an 'unchaste idolatry' of the educatee towards the educator (cf. supra), it is important also to point out the 'human, all too human humanity' of the educator. See further on the need for redemption of ethics and ethical commitment: the more radical the ethics, the more need for redemption of ethics!

In order to be sure that *amorevolezza* would not be misunderstood as sentimental love, with all its possible perversions and deviations, Don Bosco anchors it directly and completely in the love of neighbour. The affective love of *amorevolezza*, with its tangible and perceptible expressions of warmth, friendliness and conviviality should not be detached from effective love: doing good, or the commitment to do good, to children and young people. Don Bosco literally means the benevolence (*benevolenza*) that expresses itself in the good treatment (*buon trattamento*) of the young people and children entrusted to him. *Amorevolezza* runs the risk of being distorted into formalism or hypocrisy if it is not incarnated in good will and good deeds. This is undoubtedly connected to ethics that emphasises *beneficentia* (beneficence) that flows forth directly from *benevolentia*, which in its turn surpasses affective love. It ultimately concerns the doing of good to and for the other. Beneficence should not be merely external or for show but should be inspired by the will to do good. This choice of the will for the good stands at the same time for the appeal to integrate and to expand affective love. That is precisely what Don Bosco wants to emphasise with his internal linking of *amorevolezza* with '*caritas*'. [24] For that purpose he refers to the hymn to love in the first Letter to the Corinthians (1 Cor 13): "The practice of the preventive system is based entirely on the words of Saint Paul: Love is patient; it does not insist on its own way; it bears all things; hopes all things, endures all things."[25] The criteria for judging the practice of *amorevolezza* as a pedagogical treatment does not flow forth from *amorevolezza* itself, but rather from the love of neighbour which should inspire and orientate it. Thus, the educator becomes a living example of expressive love of neighbour (loving kindness) as a form of life and lifestyle for the educatee as well.

From the biblical tradition, two mutually complementary aspects of the love of neighbour can be indicated. On the one hand, there is the golden rule: "Do to others as you would have them do to you" (Matt 7:12a).[26] We can call the golden rule the minimum form of the love of neighbour. From the narrative of the Good Samaritan, on the other hand, the perspective of an exuberant but at the same time realistic and feasible love for the other is opened. Mercy that not only reveals one's being touched and moved by the suffering of the other but

24 See among others R. Biesmans, *Amorevolezza*, 31–33.

25 G. Bosco, *Il sistema preventivo*, 84/429–432. Cited by R. Biesmans, *Amorevolezza*, 32.

26 In its negative formulation: "And what you hate, do not do to anyone" (Tob 4:15a).

that also expresses itself earthily and bodily in forms of nearness and decisive assistance, and that moreover appeals to the innkeeper— a professional with provisions and organisation, namely his inn—and by means of money makes services and goods negotiable.[27] Connected to this and inspired by the last judgment in Matthew 25 (in line with Isaiah 58), the Christian tradition developed the seven bodily works of mercy: to feed the hungry, to give drink to the thirsty, to clothe the naked, to shelter the homeless, to visit the sick, to visit the imprisoned, to bury the dead. Parallel to this, the Christian tradition also developed a list of seven spiritual works of mercy: to instruct the ignorant, to counsel the doubtful, to admonish sinners, to bear wrongs patiently, to forgive offences willingly, to comfort the afflicted, to pray for the living and the dead. Unfortunately, these last seven spiritual works are now less or almost no longer known. But perhaps they offer unexpected possibilities for a Christian inspired education of *amorevolezza* anchored in caritas as love of neighbour. Six of the seven render the sensitivity of a concrete loving treatment of young people and children in all spiritual needs: to educate the weak within society and families; to assist in word and deed young people in doubt and in search of answers and not abandon them to their fate; to provide shelter, support and comfort to disadvantaged young people; to try and bring back wayward young people (truancy, alcohol and drug use, petty criminality) on the right track; to offer chances through thoughtful tolerance to unruly and difficult young people and not simply write them off; to look for forms of rehabilitation, forgiveness and reconciliation for young people who make life difficult for their educators due to their indifference or bullying and not simply send them away (cf. infra). Upon closer inspection, the spiritual works of mercy, applied to an education context, put us on the track of Salesian reasonableness. It is a way of concretising *amorevolezza* with common sense and patience with young people who, as a result of their difficult circumstances in life and psycho-affective vulnerability, do not benefit from unrelenting hardness. They require counselling that is adapted and tailored to their needs and that takes into account emotionally and practically their inabilities and abilities for growth, i.e., not only their finitude but also their infinity. This implies that *caritas* or love of neighbour is also the goal of this growth, and that it is also the means of this growth, namely

27 For further deepening in the narrative of the Good Samaritan, see among others our publication: 'Gestation of the Other in the Same. The Narrative of the Good Samaritan leads to thoughtful reflection on the soul and the embodiment of our multidimensional responsibility', in R. Burggraeve, *To Love Otherwise. Essays in Bible Philosophy and Ethics*, (Peeters: Leuven-Paris-Bristol (CT), 2020), 265–314.

through learning to practise real responsibility for the other, for example through various concrete achievable tasks and projects.

3.5.2. Pedagogical 'caritas' rooted in divine 'agapē': mercy and justice

With this, however, not everything has already been said about the anchoring of *amorevolezza* in the love of neighbour as a pedagogical inspiration, tool and objective. *Caritas* after all is in its turn rooted in the love of God: '*agapē*'. Here we arrive at the religious root of pedagogical love, both as source and as path and goal. In the Christian context, entirely in the spirit of Don Bosco, it has to do with the faith in God, the Infinite. This does not mean that whoever does not believe in God cannot experience nor substantiate the pedagogical *caritas* and *amorevolezza*, since it is about fundamental human possibilities and skills. But for a Christian, the love of neighbour in itself is not a mere human reality. It is after all the reflection and earthly realisation of its own source: the love of God for humans and the love of humans for God that ensues from it. As answer to God's love, the love of neighbour loses its first place, and it receives a responsorial structure. The love that is laid upon us, literally comes towards us, both from the other as well as from the wholly Other, immediately implies the calling not to keep that love to ourselves but to let it flow out to others. The extravagant love of God becomes the appeal and the model for the love of human persons in this world. The appeal to love our neighbour flows forth directly from the confession of faith in a God who has created us with His grace of an exuberant and totally disproportionate love (*agapē*). Or as John puts it: "Since God loved us so much, we also ought to love one another" (1 Jn 4:11) and "Those who say, 'I love God', and hate their brothers or sisters, are liars; for those who do not love a brother or a sister whom they have seen, cannot love God whom they have not seen. The commandment we have from him is this: those who love God most love their brothers and sisters also" (1 Jn 4:20-21). This implies that the Christian religion, as source and embedment of *amorevolezza*, can become a form of deep emotionality (an expression analogous to deep ecology). For Don Bosco that was unambiguously so. The deep religious emotionality of God's love wherein we are and live forms the soul and ensoulment of pedagogical love.[28] Educators are called to

---

28 In the thought, life and pedagogical deeds of Don Bosco, the Holy Virgin Mary, Immaculate Conception (8 December), Mother and Help of Christians, played an important, even essential, role. Certainly, as a form of religion that tends to the finitude of human persons (cf. supra). At the same time, the reference to Our Lady as Mother of God and our Mother can be seen as an understandable expression

imitate God's love. That makes a Christian-inspired Salesian education into a pedagogy of imitation, in the awareness that such imitation often runs through the crooked paths of imperfection and ethical failings. Moreover, we can state that the goal of education flows forth from the divinely inspired love. In and through pedagogical love, children and young people are initiated into the discovery of the meaningfulness of love and are called upon to substantiate it. For that they are presented with inspiring examples, not only the saints but also ordinary people like Mamma Margaret (Don Bosco's mother who assisted him in his pedagogical work in Turin). It is no coincidence that Don Bosco wrote for his young people accessible biographies about his paragon boys: Dominic Savio, Michael Magone, Francis Besucco.[29]

This link between love of neighbour or pedagogical love and the love of God presupposes a certain conception of God. In the Bible, God is referred to in exalted ethical terms—a unique means to indicate infinity in a qualitative way. The Infinite One in the Old Testament is spoken of and professed as the Merciful One and the Righteous One. The Hebrew root word of 'mercy'—'*rachamim*'—is '*rechem*', literally 'womb': to carry the other within oneself until the other is born, indeed: to be pregnant with the other in order to allow the other to be born. God as *Rachamim* is womb (uterus), literally 'uterinity', pregnancy, motherhood.[30] This mercy we can also call the passion of God, in the sense that the Infinite One is 'affectable' and touchable, down to One's innermost being, or rather down to One's bowels, One's mother's womb.

---

and concretisation—in the nineteenth century—of the deep emotional religiosity of God's love that creates, embraces, both heals and perfects as well as inspires and arouses every child, every youngster, every educator, every person, towards love that infinitises itself.

29 A. Giraudo (ed.), *John Bosco's Lives of Young People. Biographies of Dominic Savio, Michael Magone and Francis Besucco* Introductory essay and historical notes by Aldo Giraudo, (Roma: LAS, 2004). Cf. also: W. Collin, 'The 'educational presence' in the biographies of young people written by Don Bosco. The Salesian educator present as a help in the vocational realisation', Salesian Forum Vienna 2018: 'Like Don Bosco accompanying young people along their various paths'. Available: http://www.salesian.online/wp-content/uploads/2021/01/2018-08-22-2-Wim-Collin-The-educational-presence-in-the-biographies-of-young-people-written-by-Don-Bosco.pdf [Accessed 08/06/2022].

30 E. Levinas, *Nine Talmudic Readings*, translated and with an introduction by A. Aronowicz, (Bloomington & Indianapolis, Indiana University Press, 1994), 183.

This passivity of the sensibility by and for the other is at the same time marked by an extreme form of non-indifference, as it appears in numerous Bible stories in which the anger of God appears over inflicted injustice.[31] A God who is merciful also gets angry over the lack of mercy. A God who is love gets angry over the violation of love! The Infinite One is the most non-indifferent, because the Holy One not only takes care of the poor, the stranger, the widow and the orphan, but the One also gets agitated by the injustice that befalls those vulnerable victims. The passion for the other that animates divine mercy is undoubtedly also the same passion that drives divine justice. In this respect, we can say that the divine *agapē*, which animates human *caritas*, walks on two legs, namely mercy and justice. This also implies that pedagogical *caritas* walks equally on two legs, namely as compassion for vulnerable children and young people and as attention to the injustice done to them, daring not only to judge from indignation but also to act justly and to create conditions for this better justice (with all the tensions between mercy and justice that this entails). In this way, mercy and justice also become pedagogical goals, expressed in merciful and just forms of life and lifestyles.

In his 'gospel' (*good message*), Jesus directly affirms and reinforces the qualification of God as uterine passion for mercy and justice. He neither speaks in a neutral nor noncommittal manner about God but qualifies the One by means of linking his Name with the idea of the Kingdom of God (Mk 1:15; Lk 4:43). By 'kingdom', Jesus does not mean a place but an active event, namely the 'reign' of God. From our 'imaginary bias' (Balmary),[32] we immediately connect with the word 'reign' the ideas of power and domination, or of '*pantokrátor*' and '*omnipotens*', with which, for example, the gods in the Greek and Roman pantheon were qualified. It is therefore no coincidence that Augustine proposes to replace *omnipotens*, a representation that conjures up too much the pagan image of a 'magic god' who can do anything and intervenes again and again, with '*omni-tenens*', the 'all-encompassing': the One, the Infinite who encompasses and carries everything in his maternal womb.[33] This 'other' God strips oneself of one's dominion and majesty and omnipotence to come down and associate oneself with the misery of the miserable and stand

31 See, for example, the story of Naboth and his vineyard in 1 Kings 21: R. Burggraeve, *To Love Otherwise*, 141–202.

32 M. Philippo, 'Le biblique n'est pas accessible en solitaire: comment Balmary relit la Bible', in: *Lumen Vitae*, 56 (2001), n 4, October-December, 401–412.

33 Cf. G. Quicke, *God zegene en beware je*, (Antwerpen: Halewijn, 2017), 130.

up for that miserable other. We can also call this '*Umwertung aller Werte*' (revaluation of all values)—to use an expression of Nietzsche—an 'ethical kenosis' (self-emptying) precisely because the Infinite One disposes of oneself in order to connect with something other than oneself. "Wherever you find grandeur of the Holy One, blessed be He, you will find His humility."[34]

This humility is neither self-humiliation nor self-destruction, but a descent from the heights of the heavenly powers to join the needy and "to raise the poor from the dust… and to make them sit with princes," as we read in Psalm 113 (7–8). The Infinite, Creator-of-the-all, not only strips oneself of his omnipotence to give free space to his creatures, but the Most High also connects oneself with the powerless to raise them to strength. In this ethical kenosis, "in this descent and 'fall' of the Infinite One reveals his perfection, his elevation."[35] This also echoes in the Magnificat of Mary, who praises God for having "lifted up the humiliated" (Lk 1:52b). This goes all the way back to the heart of Hebrew revelation, namely the revelation of the Name to Moses in the burning bush: "I am I am" (*eyeh asher eyeh*) (Exod 3:14a). This Name is completely connected to His mission: "This you must say to the Israelites: the One who Is sends me to you" (Exod 3:14b). The God of the Fathers—Abraham, Isaac, and Jacob—reveals his true 'being' in the mission the One entrusts to Moses, namely, the mission to free his chosen people from the bondage of Egypt. When Moses wriggles and raises all kinds of objections, the Lord reveals his Name as the One who commits Oneself completely to His people—image of humanity-in-suffering—and the One oneself goes with Moses to deliver the people, humankind, from their misery. The biblical God is not the 'Unmoved Mover' (Aristotle)[36] but the 'Moved Mover', not a '*Deus impassibilis*' (passive God) but a '*Deus compassibilis*' (compassionate God)—an expression that Bernard of Clairvaux has bequeathed to us. The Holy One makes oneself so small, as it were, that He withdraws from his omnipotence and omniscience in order to unite Oneself with small, injured people, including the slave, to liberate and elevate them (cf. Phil 2).

This brings us to an important and at the same time remarkable insight: the paradoxical relationship between ethics and grace. It is precisely the ethics of

---

34 E. Levinas, *Is It Righteous to Be? Interviews with Emmanuel Levinas*, edited by Jill Robbins, (Stanford (CA): Stanford University Press, 2001), 282.

35 Levinas, *Is It Righteous to Be?* 282.

36 Aristotle, *Metaphysics*, 350BCE.

God that is for us grace. In Christianity, our thought on grace is determined ethically. It is thanks to the ethics of the other that we realise what grace is: that which the other signifies for us and does to us. Consequently, grace is no mere lucky coincidence of 'something that happens' but is based on the commitment of someone who turns towards us and treats us with mercy and justice, meaning to say with ethical excellence. Hence in Christianity we link grace with the love of God. "God is love", as we read in John (1 Jn 4:16), and that love befalls us as an awesome goodwill and grace: infinity as a superabundant gift. Moreover, God precedes us with his love just as John once again puts it: "In this is love, not that we loved God but that he loved us" (1 Jn 4:10; cf. 1 Jn 4:19b). The grace of God's ethics is therefore undeserved. It is proffered to us freely, without our having been able to make any claim to it beforehand.

That the other has loved us first makes us automatically think of the intergenerational relationship between parents and children, as well as the alpha and omega of all education. It is not the children who have chosen their parents and it is likewise not they who loved them first. In the children's birth and existence, they have been preceded by the love of their begetters and parents. In the relationship between the generations, love reveals itself as an asymmetry of the love that children receive because it is gifted by their parents. Only then are they able to give back love. The same fundamental structure can be found in the biblical, Jewish and Christian, religion. God is qualified as Father, as the One who gifts life: '*ex abundantia cordis*', from the abundance of the heart, as qualified infinity. But God is likewise qualified as Mother, as the Merciful One, as discussed above. This asymmetry of the love of God, Mother-Father, that befalls us as pure undeserved grace, is reflected in the parent-child relationship. It is then not coincidental that Don Bosco qualifies the educator as 'father' wherein, at the same time, he also integrates all sorts of characteristics of the 'mother'. His pedagogical love finds its source and inspiration in the infinity of God's motherly and fatherly love (*agapē*), as he expresses it over and over again like a refrain. Specifically, he does so by speaking again and again in traditional theological terms of the "divine providence", "which overwhelms us with every possible benefit", "with every good thing for body, soul and mind".[37] And again, this divine, maternal and paternal grace is for Don Bosco not only source and motivation for pedagogical

37 Biesmans, *De Magna Charta van het salesiaanse opvoedingssysteem. Hulpboekje*, 12.

love but also the supporting ground and environment in which both educator and educatee, and each human being, may live and come to fullness of life.

3.5.3. Incarnation of God's uterine love in the humane Jesus (and implications for pedagogical love)

The thought of Don Bosco on the religious inspiration (and finality) of pedagogical love, however, is no abstract thought on God but is explicitly linked with Christ, the Son of God. In the salutation of the 'Letter from Rome', both to the community of Salesians and to the boys of the Oratorio in Valdocco (Turin), he states that the words he writes "are the words of one who loves you intimately in Jesus Christ."[38]

God's *agapē* that precedes all things and brings all things to existence, is in the Christian religion still further extended in the insight and the conviction of the incarnation of God's infinite love in Jesus. "God's love was revealed among us in this way: God sent his only Son into the world so that we might live through him" (1 Jn 4:9). Consequently, it is not a formal or neutral 'modality' of God's being in this world, but an ethically qualified expression. Since God's uterinity as sensibility by-and-for-the-other is an ethically qualified modality of being, including the indignation at and condemnation of inflicted injustice, God's incarnation in and through Jesus' being, acting and speaking, can only be an ethically qualified Presence and Activity. This means that it is not the human Jesus, but the humane human Jesus, who incarnates the divine uterine *agapē*-by-and-for-the-other. Only in the humane human being Jesus do we discover the 'Christ'—the Anointed One—of God. It is the uterine passion for mercy and justice that, according to the Christian faith, comes to eruption and exaltation in the humane human Jesus: "In Christ the whole fullness of deity dwells bodily" (Col 2:9).

This has even given rise in the Christian tradition to a maternal representation of Christ, beginning with Augustine (354–430). Ambrose of Milan (337–397) also speaks of Christ carrying humanity in his womb and feeding it with spiritual milk. Anselm of Canterbury (1033–1109) calls Jesus "our mother", for he suffered more than all women during childbirth. By his death on the cross, he brought us to life. Later, female saints and mystics also refer to the

---

38 Biesmans, *De Magna Charta van het salesiaanse opvoedingssysteem. Hulpboekje*, 3.

maternal Christ. For example, the famous recluse Julian of Norwich (c. 1342–c. 1416) distinguishes in the Trinity God's fatherhood, the Son's motherhood and the Spirit's inspiration. Catherine of Siena (1347–1380) also discerns in Jesus maternal traits. We also find the maternal representation of Jesus in painting, for example 'La lamentation du Christ', a painting from the end of the 16th century preserved in L'Hôpital Notre-Dame à la Rose (Lessines, Belgium). The painting representing the dead Jesus shows not only male but also female features, namely female breasts: Jesus refers with his right hand to the nipple of his motherly left breast, indicating how he gives life through his suffering and death on the cross.[39] This maternal representation of Jesus, going beyond sex-gender-determinations, offers interesting possibilities for giving to the *amorevolezza*, as a pedagogical expression of the 'caritas', a Christological resonance, as inspiration and as a life path.

However, the fullness of God's uterine *agapē* in Jesus Christ must not be misunderstood. After all, this is an incarnated fullness, namely an earthly expression and realisation. This implies that the fullness of God's love in Jesus takes a historical, meaning contingent and finite, shape. The humanity of Jesus is not apparent, as proclaimed in the heresy of *docetism*, but real, tangible and visible in this created world. This means that Jesus' humanity is marked by the finitude with which all creatures are marked. Or as the Council of Chalcedon (451) says of Jesus Christ: "truly God and truly human". Hence Jesus reveals and gives shape to God's uterine love in a finite, imperfect way. Hence, this revelation needs further interpretation and unfolding throughout history. There is work to be done for all those who, in the wake of Jesus, allow themselves to be animated by God's *agapē*. It is a work that is never finished! This is also true of pedagogical *caritas*, which accomplishes itself as the incarnation of God's uterine mercy and justice. Even though it is animated by God's love, it accomplishes itself earthly and historically, and thus contextually. And this requires interpretation and translation and revision, again and again, in new circumstances of time and space. In other words, the real incarnational nature of pedagogical *caritas* requires the creativity of discernment in order to incarnate God's love pedagogically in the best possible way in new or

---

39 B. Debruyn, M. Vuidar, 'Une "Lamentation autour du Christ" étonnante à l'Hôpital Notre-Dame à la Rose… ou la représentation rarissime d'un Christ "maternel" datant de la fin XVIe siècle', in: E. Bocquet, R. Debruyn, G. Deleuze, C. Deplancq, C. Holvoet, A. Viatour, M. Vuidar, *L'Hôpital Notre-Dame à la Rose—De l'hôpital au musée du 3e millénaire*, (Lessines: Hôpital Notre-Dame à la Rose, 2008), 178–184.

different historical, social and cultural circumstances. This multidimensional 'inculturation', without falling into the trap of absolutising 'culturalism', must be accompanied—last but not least—by the humble insight that this work of creative interpretation and critical reinterpretation is never finished, which confirms precisely its incarnational nature! And this is true of every life form that incarnates God's love through the love of neighbour.

There is another aspect of the incarnation as the revelation of God's uterine *agapē* in and through Jesus that deserves our attention, and that is also important for the experience and discernment of pedagogical *caritas* as inspiration and lifestyle. The revelation of God's love in Jesus Christ is utterly unique and exceptional, namely because it takes place at a particular moment in history through the very corporeal man Jesus of Nazareth: "The Word became flesh and lived among us" (Jn 1:14). At the same time, this unique historical event also exhibits an exceptional character, in the sense that God's uterine passion of *agapē* no longer remains a transcendent metaphor but has tangibly and palpably, in a particular place and time, entered the world and therefore has become immanent and earthly. We cannot be surprised and amazed enough by this! But this uniqueness and particularity simultaneously exhibits a paradoxical character, in that in its uniqueness it also exhibits a dimension of 'inclusiveness'. In the words of John Paul II, "God has incarnated not only in Christ, but through Christ in all humans".[40]

The question now is what this means, including for the religious, Christian interpretation of pedagogical *caritas*, first of all as inspiration but also as life perspective. Precisely insofar as Jesus Christ in his solidarity with his people is the incarnation of the self-emptying Infinite uterine One, his being-human provides us an essential criterion for a universal understanding of God's incarnation in Christ.[41] Only a 'humane humanity', i.e., a radical association with vulnerable and injured persons, can be *le milieu divin* (divine environment), the place where God reveals and incarnates Oneself. From there

---

40 Quoted by: E. Levinas, 'La vocation de l'autre', in: E. Hirsch, *Racismes. L'autre et son visage.* (Grands entretiens réalisés par Emmanuel Hirsch), (Paris: Cerf, 1988), 96.

41 An inclusive interpretation of God's becoming human in Christ also promotes the dialogue with other religions for it can thus be acknowledged that God's love likewise seeks expression in the appearance, words and deeds of prophets and people other than Jesus, at least when authentic love—mercy and justice—is present.

we can derive that wherever this solidary humanity takes place, God's uterine *agapē* is incarnated. Everyone who substantiates the preferential 'being-for-the-vulnerable-other' of Jesus allows God and God's reign 'to be born'. That Jesus is revelation does not only mean that He incarnates and reveals God, but also that every human being who in one's life praxis associates with vulnerable and injured fellow humans makes God and God's reign present. In and through Jesus we discover this universality. Paul expresses this by calling Jesus Christ the "new Adam", namely the new divine human wherein all humans are included (Rom 5:12-21; 1 Cor 15:45-47).[42] Just like the 'old Adam' of Genesis needs to be understood inclusively as every human, the 'new Adam', Jesus, should be understand as the inclusive human. He reveals how every human person in one's finitude is the bearer of the Infinite, with that difference that Jesus was without sin and that the human person is a fallen person (cf. infra). By associating ourselves with Jesus' person, praxis and message, we see that wherever liberating humanity takes place, God becomes human and makes history. To become Christian means that we are allowed to be, and that we must be, God's incarnation. We do so in all humility, in the awareness that we always may rely on how "God's love has been poured out into our hearts through the Holy Spirit that has been given to us" (Rom 5:5).

This is particularly true of the educator's pedagogical *caritas*. A Christian educator is allowed to experience this love as living and acting 'in Christ' and as a way of making God's uterine *agapē* concrete for children and young people: incarnating a bit of the Infinite in the finite. Don Bosco understood this well. He regularly interpreted pedagogical acts as christological acts. Pedagogical love is reflected in Jesus' love. At first sight, Jesus seems to be the foremost example of all pedagogical and humane acts. Upon closer inspection, the reference to Christ becomes more than Jesus as example, this means more than an ethical interpretation of Jesus. It is also and especially about the theological significance of Jesus insofar as he makes God's infinite love present in flesh and blood, to be sure finite and imperfect but still real. According to the Christian faith the educator becomes an *alter Christus* (the other Christ). In the way in which he makes his love for children and young

---

42 See also the Vatican II Pastoral Constitution '*Gaudium et Spes*' (1965), n. 22: "Only in the mystery of the Incarnate Word does the mystery of man take on light… Christ, the new Adam, by the revelation of the mystery of the Father and his love, fully reveals man to himself and makes his supreme calling clear". Cited by Pope Francis I in his post-synodal exhortation '*Amoris Laetitia*' (2016), n. 77.

people palpable, he gives a tangible shape to God's love just as it has found its definitive and unique expression in the human Jesus. It is no coincidence that Don Bosco time and again anchored *amorevolezza* 'in Christ' and thus links it with the incarnation of God's love in Jesus. We can call this the 'mystical' and 'spiritual' soul of pedagogical love. In his 'Letter from Rome', he puts it in this way: "Jesus Christ made himself small with the little ones and he has borne our infirmities. He did not break the bruised reed and he did not quench a dimly burning wick (cf. Isa 42:3). He is your model, your Master."[43] And through the incarnated pedagogical caritas, which takes Jesus' extravagant love as an example, the educator becomes, in the flesh, for children and young people an invitation to imitate Jesus as their model and master of life!

3.5.4. Beyond the ethical Jesus: redemption of pedagogical 'caritas'

However, isn't the ethical appeal to radical love for the other, following the example of Jesus, as it bubbles up from the extravagant grace of God's uterine love, a poisoned gift?

Is the Salesian vocation to radical pedagogical caritas for vulnerable children and young people, as it flows from the gift of God's *agapē*, not a too heavy and crushing, and therefore intolerable ethical task: a mission impossible? Above, we outlined how Don Bosco, in his 'Letter from Rome' (and elsewhere), expresses his total and unrelenting commitment to his boys. It captures the imagination, and in its abundance, it is also beautiful! But isn't it too good to be true? Isn't it too much to ask? Is it even feasible for 'human humans'? This is for people who are not only finite and fragile, as we already outlined above, but also for people who fail ethically and make mistakes, for people who are—in traditional religious jargon—sinners. Educators are not ethical heroes either: they too fall short; they too sometimes prefer to be lazy rather than tired and fail the children and young people for whom they are responsible. In other words, isn't pedagogical caritas a 'stone of Sisyphus', which must be rolled upward like an impossible weight? On top of that, isn't the call to extravagant caritas, as the goal of education, also an impossible ethical task for educatees? Doesn't Jesus' gospel ask too much of people, and of young people along the way in particular? Doesn't the appeal to Jesus as an example of radical love for the other overload human ethical capacity? When

43 Biesmans, *De Magna Charta van het salesiaanse opvoedingssysteem. Hulpboekje*, 21.

ethics becomes the *'Ein und Alles'* (one and all), it chokes on its own failure and self-destruction!

This risk, this derailing of love of neighbour as responsibility by and for the other, of which Jesus is the incarnation and the excellent example, obliges us to think beyond ethics, and therefore beyond the ethical interpretation of Jesus himself. According to the Christian faith, we find this beyond ethics, this beyond the ethical Jesus, in the idea of redemption. We met this idea already above, but now it appears under a different form. In the context of human finitude, the idea of redemption appears as a response to human finitude, this being fragility, inability and imperfection. From our fragility we long for a solution to the problems that our mortality and finitude produce. We seek relief in healing and eternal life, as we saw above. But also, at the heart of uterine ethics of responsibility through and for the other arises the desire for healing and liberation. Indeed, the ethical subject not only accounts for falling short of its ethical mission of mercy and justice, and thus failing, but also for committing faults, e.g., through culpable omission, indifference or laziness, and even ill will, abuse of power or violence. Here the French philosopher Paul Ricoeur rightly makes the distinction between '*échec*' (failure) and '*faute*' (fault).[44] In the biblical tradition we call the latter 'sin'. We are not only fragile beings, insofar as we are limited and finite, but we are also ethically fallible beings, insofar as we fail to fulfil our ethical calling. Levinas points out how 'sin' is a greater 'honour' than 'weakness'.[45] For sin expresses the immanent capacity of freedom and responsibility. This is not imperfection and finitude but a form of qualitative infinity and power. In this respect, too, we can speak of '*felix culpa*' (happy guilt): happy that humans can be held ethically guilty and responsible. Happy, then, that in their actions each person does not have to be excused from one's guilt again and again, and therefore not to be considered truly free and responsible. For that would precisely reveal his misery and fragility, while his sin—oh paradox—reveals his power and greatness. It is precisely in the degradation and wounding of our ethical vocation through 'sin' or 'fault' that the desire for redemption emerges. Not in the sense that we want to be stripped of or relieved of our ethical mission, but in the sense that in the very heart and flesh of our ethical endeavours and acting we want to be healed of our 'evil', so that we can act as humanly as possible and yet remain fully ethical with and in all our ethical vulnerability and guilt.

---

44 P. Ricoeur, *Oneself as Another*, translated by Kathleen Blamey, (Chicago & London: The University of Chicago Press, 1992), 171–180, 204–218.

45 Levinas, *Totality and Infinity*, 237.

Therefore, in the Christian faith, Jesus Christ has not only an ethical meaning, namely as inspiration and example for our commitment of responsibility and uterine love, mercy and justice, he is also and above all recognised as Saviour. Too often today we experience a reduction of Christ to an 'ethical Jesus'. As the incarnation of God's uterine passion for mercy and justice, Jesus Christ is also our Redeemer and Liberator. This brings to mind our reflection above on the relationship between grace and ethics, namely that the ethics of the other is our grace. By giving himself completely, up to and including his suffering and death on the cross, Jesus, as God's Anointed One, 'redeemed' our sins of lovelessness and injustice.

> The Gospel does not say simply that the Christ takes on the world's sins and thus embodied God's love in an extravagant way, but it also says that, taking the world's sins upon his shoulders, he accordingly alleviates our burden. In other words, the Christ atones for us. His sufferings would be our recovery, as Isaiah says of his 'Servant' (Isaiah 53).[46]

Through his suffering on the cross, Jesus Christ not only meets us redemptively in our finitude, imperfection and mortality, but also heals us to the very depths of our ethical mission to bear the other in responsibility. As Saviour, he does not destroy our radical ethical mission of *caritas* but elevates it into the embrace of God's infinite *agapē*: divine grace that not only animates and inspires but also heals, transforms and completes our uterine love. It is precisely in this way that our 'mission impossible' of mercy and justice becomes possible, doable and attainable, without its radicalism being trivialised, modified or destroyed. It is precisely by touching, purifying and healing us in our ethical hearts and bodies that the redemptive Cross of Jesus, God's Christ (Anointed One), enables us to live up to and endure our vocation and mission of ethical uterinity, not only in spite of all our failures (imperfections) but also in spite of—and through—our 'sinful' faults against merciful and righteous love. The ethics of the other, namely Jesus the Christ, is our grace: not only source of inspiration but also source of healing. The love of the divine other, as it became visible and tangible in Jesus, is our liberation. The fragile and wounded heart of our ethical mission of love is so touched, healed and transformed by the ethics of the other, Jesus the Anointed One of God, right down to the *de profundis* (from the depths) of our 'womb' that it burgeons again and again into a real uterine passion for mercy and justice by trial and error.

---

46 P. Nemo, *Job and the Excess of Evil* (with a postface by Emmanuel Levinas, Tr. M. Kigel), (Pittsburgh, PE: Dusquesne University Press, 1998), 193.

3.5.5. Divine forgiveness that heals the ethical heart and flesh of humans

The vision of Jesus Christ as Saviour implies the idea of divine forgiveness healing the ethical heart of people. This idea appears frequently in the Bible as a prominent figure of the divine *Rachamim.* It belongs, according to Paul Ricoeur, to the "*économie du don*" (economy of the gift), in the sense that it is a gratuitous gift that transcends any utilitarian calculation.[47] The Merciful One always regrets denounced calamity, as for example the prophet Jonah expresses it to his deep disappointment. Though he could hardly bear it, he had to recognise that the Infinite One was moved to compassion by the Ninevites, the archenemies of Israel, when they were willing to "turn from their evil ways and from the violence that is in their hands" (Jon 3:8). This leads him to one of the most beautiful, contradictory confessions of God's mercy in the Bible: "For I knew that You are a gracious God and merciful, slow to anger, and abounding in steadfast love, and ready to relent from punishing" (Jon 4:2b). This does not undo his judgement—to be distinguished from vengeance—but it does lift it above itself. Again and again, the Infinite One offers his forgiving mercy, not only after sin and guilt committed, but also as a promise "that all things will be made new" (see above and also below). The Psalms, too, lyrically express how divine forgiveness is a promise that stands as a rock, a rock and a beacon of light, for God himself is "my rock in whom I take refuge" (Ps 18:2), "my fortress; for you are my refuge" (Ps 31:3.4); in short, a safe refuge, but also an unshakable foundation: "He is the rock, a faithful God, without deceit" (Deut 32:4). We can also call it the unconditional character of divine forgiveness precisely because it precedes as offer and gift all conversion of the guilty. Because God loved us first (1 Jn 4:19), His forgiveness also precedes our ethical commitment and our attempt to forgive. In this respect, philosopher Jacques Derrida is right when he says that forgiveness is exceptional and excessive and therefore exceeds any form of *do-ut-des* (I give, so that you may give).[48] It cannot be the result of deliberation and negotiation. Forgiveness can never be demanded or enforced. Again, in Ricoeur's words: "its logic is that of abundance which distinguishes love from the logic of reciprocity in justice".[49]

---

47 P. Ricoeur, *La mémoire, l'histoire, l'oubli,* (Paris: Seuil, 2000), 625–630. [English translation by K. Blamey & D. Pellauer: *Memory, History, Forgetting,* (Chicago: University Chicago Press, 2004)].

48 J. Derrida, *On Cosmopolitanism and Forgiveness,* (London & New York: Taylor & Francis Ltd. – Routledge, 2001).

49 P. Ricoeur, *La mémoire, l'histoire, l'oubli,* 622.

The question now is how this 'abundant gift' of divine forgiveness brings about healing and liberation in the guilty person. After all, the evil done appears at first glance to be definitive, namely that it cannot be undone.[50] This implies that forgiveness—even divine forgiveness—cannot apply to the evil done. Only the one who inflicts the evil can be forgiven! Well, on closer inspection, forgiveness acts on the guilty person in such a way that he or she is no longer identified with his or her evil. In the logical order of things, the evil that someone inflicts on another sticks to the perpetrator in such a way that he irreversibly subscribes with it: 'once a thief, always a thief'. This clinging to one's own wrong deed is dramatic because it crushes the guilty person. Hence the longing for, or rather the plea for, deliverance. Well, the paradox of forgiveness is that it fully recognises the evil done and the responsibility of the guilty person yet does not fix and cement the perpetrator in it forever (as Lot's wife turned into a lump of salt forever) (Gen 19:26). The forgiveness creates distance between the guilty person and his evildoing, space is created to breathe again and become 'new'. Levinas labels this a 'resurrection event'.[51] For forgiveness acts directly on the definitive character of the act, by stripping it of its irreversibility, without, however, fleeing from it. In this sense, it is literally liberating the guilty person from the reduction of guilt: "the non-definitiveness of the definitive; an ever-recommencing alterity of the accomplished".[52] Forgiveness restores the irredeemable and recalls the irrevocable. She liberates us from the despair that is entwined with the unchangeable. At the moment when all is lost, she makes all possible again. Through forgiveness, the person receiving forgiveness is torn out of the bondage to his deed and transformed in such a way that, remaining the same, he nevertheless becomes a different and new, reborn human being. The forgiveness is literally a 're-naissance', a 'rebirth': the guilty person can start afresh, literally rise (which is exactly the resurrection as 'getting up', 'standing up', 'rising'). Forgiveness is not a reward for some effort, but the utterly gratuitous gift that touches and affects the guilty person in his guilt in such a way that, not in spite of but because of this guilt, he becomes a different person. The loving promise of forgiveness does not announce a simple future in which the weight of guilt is counterbalanced or compensated for by some emancipation, such as forgetting or apology, for example. On the contrary, it announces a future in which the present—the enchainment in guilt—is literally

50 Levinas, *Totality and Infinity*, 281–282.

51 E. Levinas, *Existence and Existents*, Tr. A. Lingis, (The Hague: Martinus Nijhoff, 1978), 92.

52 Levinas, *Totality and Infinity*, 283.

're-called'. This re-call recognises the evil done, the harm done, without taking anything away from it. Yet it does not leave this evil untouched, it resists its destructive fatality for the perpetrator. Forgiveness is the restoration of the irreparable, the revocation of the irrevocable. The guilty person is redeemed from his guilt precisely by acknowledging this guilt but not by shackling the guilty person in it forever. In this respect, (divine) forgiveness as liberation is the absolute antipode of hell, which essentially consists in solidifying the guilty person in his guilt forever and ever: an irreversible doom, which is precisely what damnation is.[53] "The pardoned being is not the innocent being. The difference does not justify placing innocence above pardon; it permits the discerning in pardon of a surplus of happiness, the strange happiness of reconciliation, the *felix culpa*, given in an everyday experience which no longer astonishes us",[54] "the surplus reconciliation provides by reason of the rupture it integrates."[55]

Yet this deliverance does not happen automatically, without input from the guilty party. On the contrary, divine forgiveness is not only unconditional but also conditional. It does not become real if the guilty person shifts his responsibility away from himself in all sorts of forms of denial, 'de-culpabilisation' or rationalisation and self-deception,[56] or degrades to his fragility, imperfection, finitude: 'I couldn't do anything about it! It was stronger than me'; or: 'My hormones, my familial or social conditioning played a part in me'; or still: 'I am not a perpetrator but a victim of my past!' The gift of healing forgiveness can only work if the guilty person honestly accepts and acknowledges their responsibility and guilt for the harm done and expresses it authentically.[57] This is precisely the conditional side of divine forgiveness (and of any forgiveness, including that between human beings, which Pope Francis also speaks about in his encyclical *Fratelli tutti*).[58] Desmond Tutu rightly says:

> Confessing is not easy. We all know how difficult it is for most of us to admit that we have done wrong. Perhaps nothing in the world is that difficult—in

53 Levinas, *Existence and Existents*, 89–92.

54 Levinas, *Totality and Infinity*, 283.

55 Ibid., 284.

56 D. Pollefeyt, *Ethics after the Holocaust*, (Leuven-Paris-Bristol (CT): Peeters Publishers, 2018), 173–174.

57 J. Monbourquette & I. d'Aspremont, *Demander pardon sans s'humilier?* (Paris-Montréal: Bayard, Novalis, 2004).

58 Pope Francis, *Fratelli tutti. On Fraternity and Social Friendship*, Assisi, tomb of St Francis, (October 3, 2020), nn. 236–254

> almost every language, the most difficult words are, "I'm sorry". Therefore, it is not surprising that those who are accused of heinous acts... almost always look for a way out to avoid admitting that they were indeed capable of committing such acts.[59]

Authentic confession is quite a work because one must not only acknowledge that one has done harm and injustice to another, but also accept that this harm must be settled ('paid back') and that the victim is entitled to it. The recognition of wrongdoing and one's own part in it must also take place as regret and remorse for the harm done, in the honest emotional realisation that irreparable harm may have been done to the victim (and others to whom the victim is closely related). Furthermore, repentance becomes effective only when an offender is willing to repair the damage done, if possible. In any case, he must promise, and commit from that promise, not to do the harm committed again. This specifically requires a different lifestyle, a different way of taking responsibility for the other. This requires a purification of the ethical subject, the responsible guilty person.

The forgiveness due to the other, particularly to the divine other, creates the space and the resilience for this. Indeed, there is something peculiar about divine forgiveness as a gift and promise. After all, on the basis of memory and judgment, pardon not only demands confession (including repentance and purification as transformation), but it also makes confession possible. Only the one who knows and can expect that she or he will be forgiven is capable of confessing, and then not only verbally and formally but wholeheartedly and thoroughly. If the perpetrator or 'sinner' knows in advance that there is no chance of compassion and forgiveness, he will do everything in his power to get out from under the blame or to cover it up or even to justify his actions (e.g., as a form of smallest unavoidable evil). Only the unconditional promise of forgiveness frees the guilty person to stand honestly in their guilt and responsibility, without being driven back into themselves and crushed by that guilty liability. This is also the thesis of Hannah Arendt who describes forgiveness as a promise precisely in order to keep open for the perpetrator (and for the victim) of inflicted evil healing and renewal.[60] In this respect,

59 D. Tutu, *Geen toekomst zonder verzoening*, (Amsterdam: De Bezige Bij, 1999), 257–258 (AT). [English edition: *No Future without Forgiveness*, (London: Transworld Publisher, 2000)].

60 H. Arendt, *The Human Condition*, (London-Chicago: The University of Chicago Press, 1958), 233–247.

divine forgiveness as promise and healing grace brings about a discontinuity in time. We already saw how forgiveness unbinds the fatal and irreversible character of the action by releasing the guilty person from the enchainment to his past. At the same time—and this is the paradox of forgiveness as a promise—forgiveness institutes permanence and reliability, and thus future. As offer and promise, the guilty person knows that there is still a future, that everything about his life has not yet been said, and that he may also have confidence about that future. Every promise is an attempt to find an answer to the uncertainty of existence—uncertainty that arises from both the self and the others. There is so much that constantly escapes, making the future seem like a lottery ticket. The promise, for which the one who utters it gives guarantees, consists precisely in creating in this darkness—of myself and others—an 'island' of stability and confidence. The guilty person may and can dare to raise oneself above oneself from one's guilt and bring this guilt—by confession and expression of regret—before the face of the divine other. From his gratuitous promise and abundant gift of forgiveness, the infinite Other is not only open to the guilty but also heals and frees him, making him new, — remaining the same, becoming an 'other', as we indicated above. Of course, this gift to the guilty also implies the ethical task of forgiving others their debt. Divine forgiveness is not a cheap but an appealing forgiveness, as Jesus still puts it: "Be merciful, just as your Father is merciful" (Lk 6:36).

This emphasis on interhuman forgiveness also shows, last but not least, the originality of Jesus' view of forgiveness.[61] For him it is clear that it is not only in the power of God to forgive, but that this power is also given to human beings as an original, and not as a derived, power. Besides, interhuman forgiveness constitutes a condition of divine forgiveness (cf. Matt 18:35; Mk 11:25; Matt 6:14-15). This does not alter the unconditional character of divine forgiveness, but it means that God makes his forgiveness dependent on the condition of human forgiveness. Whoever does not forgive his brother or sister with all his heart and flesh cannot receive God's forgiveness, as it states in the Lord's Prayer: "Forgive us our debts, as we also have forgiven our debtors" (Matt 6:12). In this way Jesus connects the unconditional gift of God's forgiveness with the condition of forgiving other people. Without interpersonal forgiveness, there is no divine forgiveness!

61 Cf. H. Arendt, *The Human Condition*, 238–239.

introduces in the one confessing the awareness of their human responsibility and thus of their human freedom and responsibility that can be applied to either good or evil. Here the confession broaches the dimension of infinity in the (young) person. In that way, both the Sacrament of Confession as well as the reconciliation rite surpass the thought on mere finitude that reduces all failings of the person to a form of failure and a form of imperfection whereby the ethical is actually eliminated. In fact, moral failing, in Christian terms 'sin', is a stronger confirmation of human dignity than the emphasising of human imperfection. By means of this infinity, which especially marks our corporeality, we are vulnerable so that our capacity for freedom and responsibility itself is threatened. Then again, our moral failing confirms that we are free and responsible beings. And that is precisely the dimension of infinity in our finitude! There is no guilt without accountability, without free self-determination in order to be called to give justification. That we are able to do evil points to our human dignity, our being image-of-God, more than to the awareness that we can fail or remain beneath the measure of our task.[66]

Still, the human person should not be reduced to one's moral responsibility and guilt, for that leads to moral overburdening and burnout. A moralistic view of the human that puts emphasis especially on the examination of conscience, guilt and confession, reduces the human person to one's ethical dynamism. Even though Don Bosco stressed this dimension, at the same time he discovered, on the basis of his strong supernatural conviction, the aspect of God's mercy as grace in the Sacrament of Confession. The need to go beyond the ethical (literally the desire for the 'trans-ethical') is present in the ethically living person: the sublimation of the person into a transcending space wherein one is healed of one's guilt without destroying the possibility of one's being guilty. That is precisely the forgiveness that is proffered of which the confession is an intensified, sacramental expression but not the only expression. Thanks to God's forgiveness, the Infinite no longer remains external but rather descends to the finite in order to raise it from its finitude above itself into infinity, precisely by means of healing the human freedom and responsibility.

It is and remains pedagogically meaningful to give young people the chance to associate their growing freedom and responsibility with forgiveness and reconciliation in general (cf. supra), and with the Sacrament of Confession

66 Levinas, *Totality and Infinity*, 237.

and sacramentals of reconciliation in particular. In that way, their ethical development is not only confirmed but also lifted up beyond itself: gift and task thanks to that gift. Thanks to divine forgiveness, the Infinite One descends into the soul of the finite and sinful person, whereby the guilty one is lifted up beyond her or his ethical fragility and thus gives expression to the Infinite. The final word is not given to ethics, but to the 'trans-ethical' that surpasses ethics and likewise provides a future: divine forgiveness as a recreating infinity. This relationship between grace and ethics is of vital importance for a balanced education. I am not the alpha and omega; everything is given to me. That does not mean that I am able to live only in indolent surrender. What is given to me likewise includes the task to give in turn to others what I have received. There is no ethics without grace that both precedes and follows freedom and responsibility. But there is also no grace without ethics, for otherwise the gifted infinity remains invisible and ineffective in finitude.

3.7. Final Redemption as Ethical and Educational Awakening

Our reflection on the sacramental mediation of God's love made it possible to accord the Christian idea of redemption its proper place in education. In the conviction that only in this way can justice be done to our starting view on religion as a child of poverty and wealth. On the one hand, the poverty of finitude and moral vulnerability leads to the desire for salvation that brings the redeemed person to fullness. On the other, the wealth of infinity leads, on the basis of love, to a unique form of poverty, i.e., to the awareness that this love is not loving enough and propels towards "a hunger which increases itself, infinitely".[67]

With this, however, not everything has been said about the relationship between ethics and redemption (grace). In the Christian faith, mention is indeed also made of an ultimate salvation or eschatology. In supernaturalist jargon, this is about the last things: death, judgment, hell and heavenly glory. Our destination is heaven, that was Don Bosco's deepest conviction. Our ultimate goal is union with God in the afterlife. We are on our way to the eternal bliss along the path of an ethically excellent life, supported by the sacraments and helped by a warm devotion to Mary.

67 Levinas, *Humanism of the Other*, 30.

Just like the idea of salvation, eschatology, understood as the end-time, can also be interpreted positively. Jesus' profession of faith in God indeed implies a goal and orientation for human acts. When people profess faith in the God of Jesus, they can only do so in truth if they act in agreement with the deepest being of the Infinite One. This means in the direction of the reign of love, mercy and justice—the qualified forms of its infinity. Whoever desires to follow Jesus can only choose for the ethical good against evil, suffering and injustice in all its forms. Not just anything is good. Only that which proceeds in the direction of God's lordship is good. Believing in the God of Jesus is not possible within indifference or neutrality. It requires involvement in our fellow humans. Whatever happens in this world in terms of suffering, evil and injustice should not leave us unmoved. It demands from us to go against evil and to commit ourselves to the good, in the direction of God's grand dream: His reign. This is about the fulfilment of God's being infinite love, mercy and justice, until God has become all in all thanks to His uterine grace.

For a Christian inspired education, this means that the reference to and the initiation in the eschatological perspective of the faith can never lead to ethical indifference or half-heartedness. On the contrary, education with and from 'the last things', to use Don Bosco's traditional language, provokes. It calls us to make a difference in this world between justice and injustice, between mercy and abuse of power, between truth and falsehood, between faithfulness and unfaithfulness, between peace and war. That qualitative value-difference likewise applies to education as relationship, system and provision. Not every form of education is equally humane, equally acceptable, equally good or good enough. The linking of eschatology and ethics makes it possible to appreciate the ethical dimension of traditional supernaturalism and at the same time to broaden it. The perspective of the afterlife surpasses not only our inner-worldly existence but likewise implies an appeal to an inner-worldly commitment. That commitment should not be interpreted individualistically as 'earning my heaven'. Striving for one's own salvation beyond death must be opened up to the salvation of the others in community. It concerns, in other words, not a solipsistic but a relational and holistic infinity. Our salvation is not separate from but finds precisely its place in and through the world as human milieu and as creation. We can link this socioecological broadening of salvation, and consequently also of ultimate salvation, with what Don Bosco formulates succinctly as the goal of education, already cited above: the formation of honest citizens and good Christians (*onesti cittadini e buoni*

Cristiani). Whoever wants to be a 'good Christian' and whoever believes in heaven and the afterlife must commit oneself ethically to become 'an honest and honourable citizen' within the family and society, and likewise for that purpose to create a good environment on earth. We can call this the paradox of a true Christian education: to believe in heaven, God's infinity, means for humans that they (to be sure, finite and fallible) incarnate God's love in this world whereby they at the same time anticipate the promise of the coming eternal, full life. No heavenly transcendent infinity without an incarnated infinity in the finitude of this earthly world!

A 'Pro-Vocative' Dialogical Conclusion

In conclusion to our anthropological-theological reflection on *religione* as an essential pillar in Don Bosco's view on education, we would like to pose a critical note on the way in which today, in our secularised and post-Christian society, the dimension of the Christian faith in various educational projects of a Christian signature are replaced by the more general and vague perspective on meaning detached from distinct ideological and religious incarnations. With that, it indeed acknowledges that in human existence lies a striving for meaning and spirituality, but the Christian-confessional profile is set aside. Or stronger still, this characteristic is found to be irrelevant for it is only an expression of a private opinion that possesses no force of communicability anymore and no longer has any social and cultural relevance. This happens because people no longer believe in it or because its clients are far distanced from it or have become too pluralistic in composition. A Salesian education project that only takes to heart the creation of meaning and spirituality in general and synchronises its concrete expression to be 'in tune' with the client can actually not be called a Don Bosco project anymore. For Don Bosco, religion has a clear Christian profile after all. Meaning is not obtainable in itself, detached from a concrete particularity and a set of convictions. Or rather, Christianity is only accessible as a particular form of searching for and of finding meaning.

For Salesian youth ministry and education, that is no incidental matter. Hence the anchoring of the pedagogical *amorevolezza* (and *ragione*) in the biblical love of neighbour (*caritas*) and in God's uterine love (*agapē*) forms part of the Salesian identity. This uniqueness must manifest itself in concrete forms and shapes, symbols and rituals, feasts and traditions, convictions and views. Precisely in our secularising post-confessionality, a reprofiling out of one's own uniqueness is necessary without annulling one's own individuality into an inclusive universality, namely into the only and full truth that labels other truths as untruths or reduces them to oneself as parts of one's own truth. It is not only the attention to meaning but specifically to Christian meaning as well, without lapsing into fundamentalist narrowness, that remains more than ever a task. Out of a Christian identity, anchored in the love of neighbour and God's uterine love in Christ outlined above, one stands open for the 'other': those of other faiths and convictions, the non-believers, the fragmented still-barely-believers, the indifferent a-believers. That respect and that acknowledgement, however, cannot mean that one smooths away and reduces one's own Christian profile as if one should be embarrassed by it. The dialogue *ad extra*, with those of other ideologies, i.e., the interconvictional dialogue, requires the dialogue *ad intra*: the loyal, at the same time critical, conversation with one's own Christian tradition. An open-minded, at the same time humble and self-critical, profiling of one's own Christian specificity is more honest than a vague and general reference to meaning and spirituality, whereby one then still sneaks in stealthily one's own distinctiveness. In this latter case, one no longer really knows what one can expect, while in the former, one is transparent with a distinctly unique Christian offer without standing in the way of the openness for the other and the stranger. Only in this way does a qualified tolerance become possible: this is a huge challenge for the future of the Salesian institutions and pedagogical projects.